TOURING
Central England

visit **Britain**
publishing

Published by VisitBritain Publishing
Thames Tower, Blacks Road, London W6 9EL

First published 2006

© British Tourist Authority (trading as VisitBritain) 2006

Maps reproduced by kind permission of Ordnance Survey on behalf of HMSO.
© Crown copyright 2006. All rights reserved. Ordnance Survey Licence number 100040235.

ISBN 0 7095 8281 1
Product code: TOURG02

A CIP catalogue record for this book is available from the British Library.

The information contained in this publication has been published in good faith on the basis of information submitted to VisitBritain and is believed to be correct at time of going to press. Nevertheless, VisitBritain regrets that it cannot guarantee complete accuracy and all liability for loss, disappointment, negligence or other damages caused by reliance on the information contained in this publication, is hereby excluded.

As changes also often occur after press date, it is advisable to confirm information and any special requirements before your visit. We would be grateful if you would advise us of any inaccuracies you identify.

Produced for VisitBritain Publishing by Departure Lounge Limited
Contributing authors: Etain O'Carroll, Roger St Pierre, Andrew Stone
Cartography: Draughtsman Maps; pages 8-9: Cosmographics
Reprographics by Blaze Creative
Printed and bound in the UK by Butler and Tanner

Jacket: View down Cotswolds country lane

Title page: Horsey Windpump, Norfolk Broads; **Pages6-7**: Punting on the River Cam, Cambridge; **Pages 10-11**: Horsey Windmill, Norfolk; **Pages 50-51**: Edenham, Lincolnshire; **Pages 74-75**: Burford Church, Oxfordshire; **Pages 108-109**: The Iron Bridge at Ironbridge, Shropshire

TOURING
Central England

TWENTY SPECIALLY CREATED DRIVING ITINERARIES

Published by VisitBritain

Contents

Norfolk, Suffolk, Essex, Hertfordshire, Cambridgeshire and Bedfordshire

Lincolnshire, Nottinghamshire, Leicestershire, Rutland and Northamptonshire

Berkshire, Oxfordshire, Buckinghamshire and Gloucestershire

Warwickshire, Worcestershire, Herefordshire and Shropshire

Central England

For centuries the rolling countryside, big skies and charming villages of Central England have attracted writers, academics and royalty alike. Our tours of the region will guide you through this economic powerhouse, from the gorgeous medieval wool towns of the Cotswolds and East Anglia to the redbrick warehouses and orderly canals of the Industrial Revolution. Visit the ancient university towns of Cambridge and Oxford, traipse the hills that inspired Shakespeare and Elgar or explore the dreamy castles and mansions that litter this heartland of English heritage.

Specialist travel writers have crafted the 20 guided driving tours in this book to cover circular routes of two to four days, which include famous and lesser-known sights alike. The itineraries can be joined at any point along the way or easily linked to shape a longer journey, and where appropriate, each itinerary also suggests ways to extend your trip with scenic walks, tours on heritage railways and boat trips.

A PROMISE OF QUALITY

We have not included specific details in this guide of places to stay on your short break in England, but you will find a wide choice of places to stay across the region. Choosing somewhere displaying the Enjoy England Quality Rose ensures you know what to expect and can book with confidence.

The following tourist board websites will provide you with detailed information on where you can stay and eat in the areas covered by this guide, as well as other useful travel advice.

www.enjoyengland.com
www.enjoyenglandseastmidlands.com
www.visitbritain.com
www.visiteastofengland.com
www.visittheartofengland.com

The Tours

The book comprises four colour-coded chapters divided by county, each of which contains between four and six tours. Each tour follows the route plotted on the map, giving short descriptions of places of interest along the way. Feature boxes highlight additional information such as literary links and walks. A final box suggests places off the tour route that, with a little more time, are worth a detour. Remember, in larger towns and cities and at popular attractions, it's a good idea to use park-and-ride schemes where they are provided.

Introduction
Each tour has a short introduction that gives a flavour of the area covered by the tour route.

Tour map
Each route is plotted on the tour map in blue. Blue numbered bullets correspond to the number of each entry and the name is labelled in blue. Places mentioned in the 'with more time' box are also labelled in blue – and where located off the map, are arrowed off.

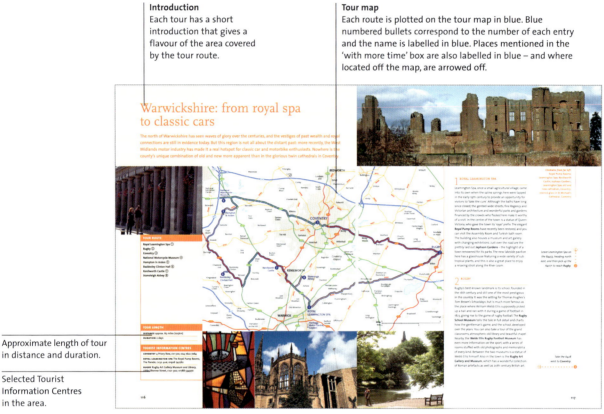

Approximate length of tour in distance and duration.

Selected Tourist Information Centres in the area.

Entry description
Each numbered entry explores the area's most important attractions.

Directions
A suggested route between consecutive entries is provided. You might also like to use a full road atlas to check minor roads.

Feature boxes
The story behind selected places; literary and historical links; local legends and heroes; or suggested walks and cycle rides.

Picture captions
Each image has a caption; boxed images are explained in the relevant box.

With more time box
This offers suggestions for places and attractions that are off the route but worth exploring if you have more time.

CENTRAL ENGLAND

North Sea

The Wash

The Broads

pages 52-57
pages 58-63
pages 64-69
pages 12-19
pages 20-25
pages 26-31
pages 44-49
pages 38-43
pages 32-37
pages 116-119
pages 70-73
pages 132-137
pages 120-125
pages 110-115
pages 126-131
pages 102-107
pages 94-101
pages 88-93
pages 82-87
pages 76-81

NEWCASTLE UPON TYNE
SUNDERLAND
MIDDLESBROUGH
Whitby
Northallerton
Malton
YORK
LEEDS
Selby
KINGSTON UPON HULL
ROTHERHAM
SHEFFIELD
Worksop
Sherwood Forest
Mansfield
Newark-on-Trent
NOTTINGHAM
DERBY
STOKE-ON-TRENT
GRIMSBY
Market Rasen
Mablethorpe
LINCOLN
Skegness
Boston
LINCOLNSHIRE
NOTTINGHAMSHIRE
Wells-next-the-Sea
Cromer
NORFOLK
NORWICH
Great Yarmouth
Lowestoft
Thetford Forest
Thetford
Southwold
Melton Mowbray
LEICESTERSHIRE
Oakham
LEICESTER
Stamford
PETERBOROUGH
Market Harborough
CAMBRIDGESHIRE
Ely
Bury St Edmunds
SUFFOLK
Aldeburgh
Orford Ness
Shrewsbury
Ironbridge
WOLVERHAMPTON
WALSALL
SUTTON COLDFIELD
Bridgnorth
Church Stretton
BIRMINGHAM
WEST MIDLANDS
COVENTRY
Rugby
Kettering
NORTHAMPTONSHIRE
Huntingdon
Newmarket
CAMBRIDGE
Ludlow
SOLIHULL
Kenilworth
Royal Leamington Spa
Rushden
NORTHAMPTON
Bedford
Droitwich
WORCESTER
Alcester
WARWICKSHIRE
Stratford-upon-Avon
Towcester
Leominster
Pershore
Evesham
Royston
Saffron Walden
Sudbury
Hay-on-Wye
Hereford
Great Malvern
WORCESTERSHIRE
Banbury
Buckingham
BEDFORDSHIRE
STEVENAGE
COLCHESTER
The Naze
Tewkesbury
Chipping Norton
LUTON
Witham
Mersea Island
Maldon
GLOUCESTER
CHELTENHAM
Bourton-on-the-Water
Aylesbury
BUCKINGHAMSHIRE
HERTFORDSHIRE
Hertford
ESSEX
IPSWICH
Forest of Dean
Stroud
Burford
OXFORD
Abingdon
HEMEL HEMPSTEAD
ST ALBANS
CHELMSFORD
GLOUCESTERSHIRE
OXFORDSHIRE
Didcot
Henley-on-Thames
Marlow
WATFORD
LONDON
BASILDON
SOUTHEND-ON-SEA
SWINDON
Windsor
SLOUGH
BERKSHIRE
READING
GILLINGHAM
BRISTOL
BATH
WOKING
BASINGSTOKE
MAIDSTONE
CRAWLEY
RDIFF

Miles 0   50
Kms 0   50

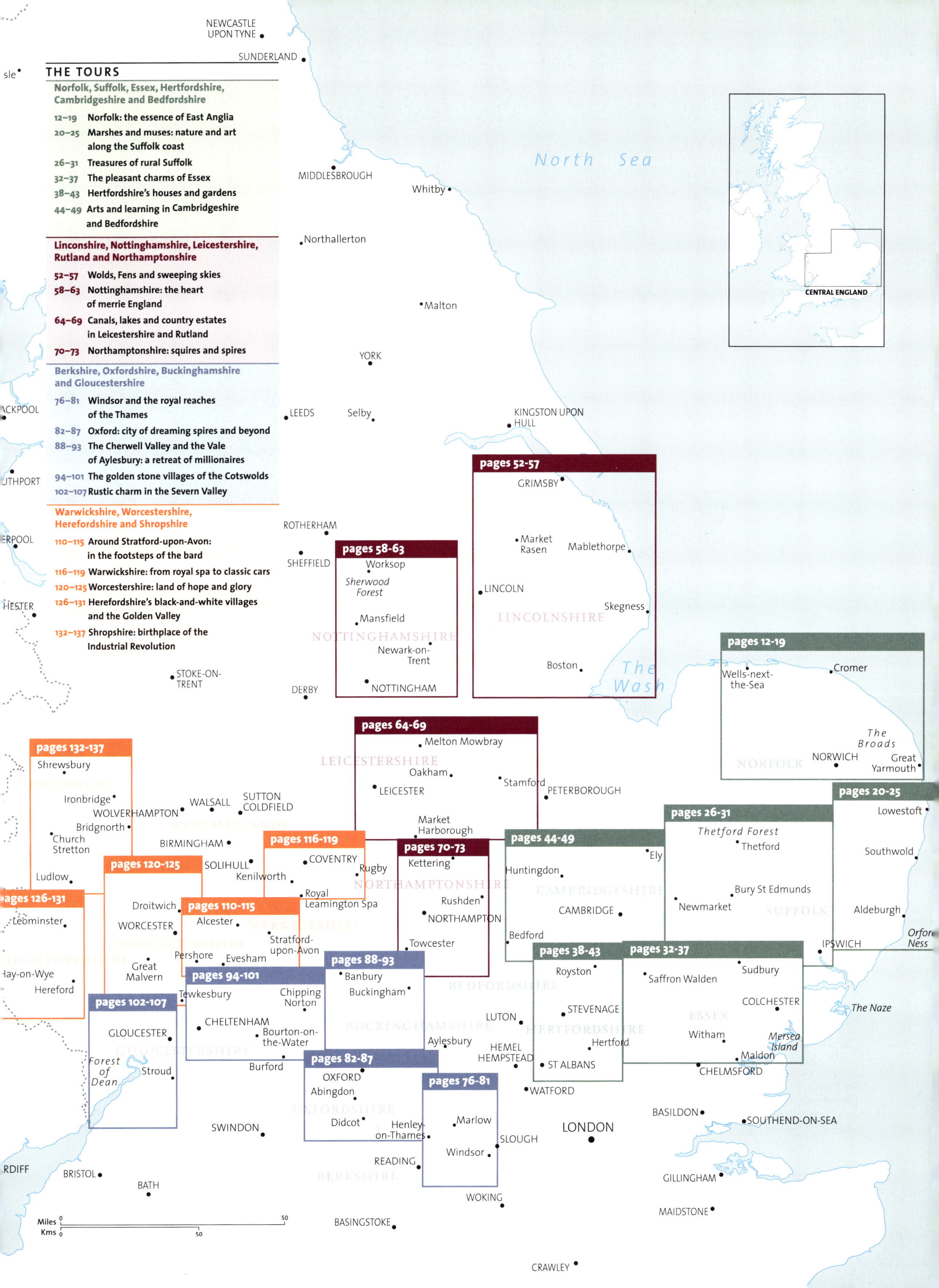

Norfolk, Suffolk, Essex, Hertfordshire, Cambridgeshire and Bedfordshire

Norfolk: the essence of East Anglia

Norfolk is a place of marshes and meres, lonely, dune-fringed beaches, lively seaside resorts and picturesque villages set amid vast swathes of agricultural land in a big-sky landscape. It's not all as flat as you might expect – up towards the north coast are a succession of steep little hills that offer sweeping North Sea views. Brick and flint are the favoured building materials in these parts, and they lend a rustic air to the quaintly named towns and hamlets. Then there's the fine city of Norwich, an eternal hive of activity, with its rich inheritance of churches, impressive castle and the soaring spire of its landmark cathedral.

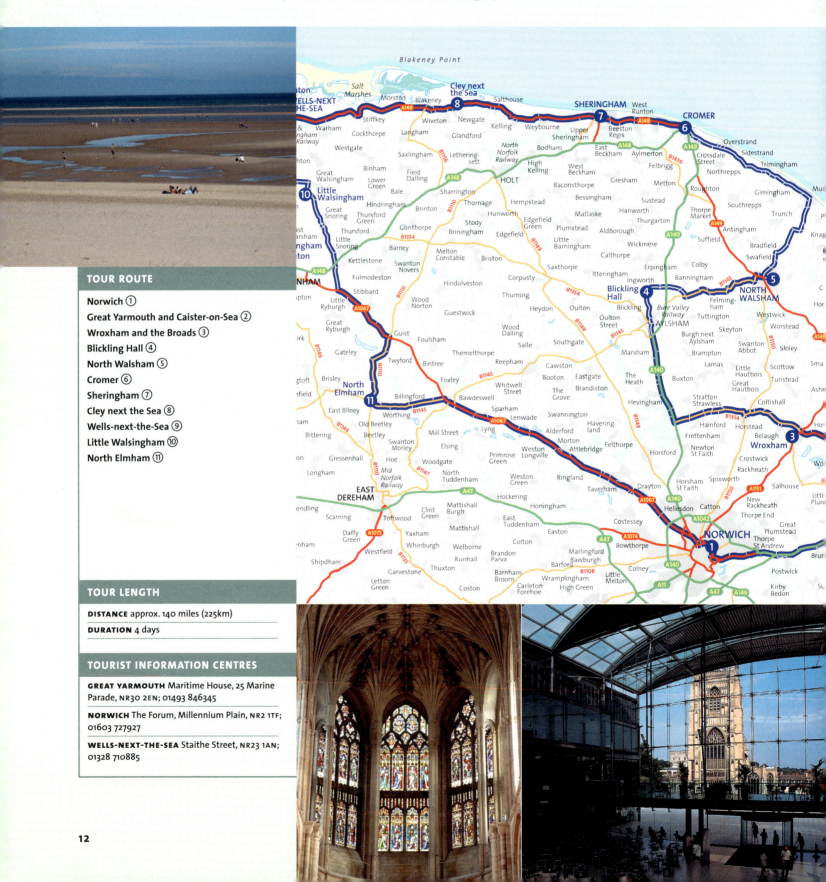

TOUR ROUTE

Norwich ①
Great Yarmouth and Caister-on-Sea ②
Wroxham and the Broads ③
Blickling Hall ④
North Walsham ⑤
Cromer ⑥
Sheringham ⑦
Cley next the Sea ⑧
Wells-next-the-Sea ⑨
Little Walsingham ⑩
North Elmham ⑪

TOUR LENGTH

DISTANCE approx. 140 miles (225km)

DURATION 4 days

TOURIST INFORMATION CENTRES

GREAT YARMOUTH Maritime House, 25 Marine Parade, NR30 2EN; 01493 846345

NORWICH The Forum, Millennium Plain, NR2 1TF; 01603 727927

WELLS-NEXT-THE-SEA Staithe Street, NR23 1AN; 01328 710885

Clockwise from far left:
beach, Wells-next-the-Sea;
Cley next the Sea; shopping
arcade, Norwich; foyer of the
Forum building, Norwich;
Norwich Cathedral

1 NORWICH

Norfolk's county town is a wondrous place, prettily set on steep hills rising from the banks of the River Wensum. It was a haven for Protestants fleeing persecution on the Continent during the 16th and 17th centuries, and at one time more than a third of its population was made up of immigrants from Flanders and France. This meant that the city was staunchly Parliamentarian during the Civil War – a factor that assured the near-intact survival of its medieval core.

There are more medieval churches per capita here than anywhere else in England – more than 30 in total, though many of that number now serve a more secular purpose. The 900-year-old **cathedral** boasts England's largest monastic cloisters and its second-tallest spire. There are also more than 1,000 beautiful roof bosses and, in the cathedral's library, 7,000 rare books, including many of the first to be printed in England. To the south west of the cathedral, the mighty **castle** keep, built in Norman times, has been recently refurbished. Besides the dark, brooding dungeons, it contains galleries displaying beautiful landscape paintings by the 19th-century Norwich School of painters, plus, quaintly, the world's largest collection of teapots. Across from the castle is the **Royal Norfolk Regimental Museum**, which tells the story of this unit from its beginnings in 1685. Nearby, the **Colman's Mustard Shop and Museum** records the 200-year history of this favourite condiment, and offers you the chance to taste a selection of different mustards.

Located in the city's bustling shopping district, the ultra-modern, horseshoe-shaped **Forum** building was built to replace the historic library destroyed by fire in 1994. A multi-use social and cultural centre, it houses a vast library, a tribute to the US air crews stationed in Norwich during World War II, and 'Origins' – an exploration of 2,000 years of local history, spread over three floors and featuring an impressive photo gallery and a film show. There's also an outdoor skating rink here each winter.

Established 900 years ago, Norwich open-air **market** claims to be the largest in Europe. It is still a bustling affair, and a good place to try the local fast-food speciality: peas with mint sauce. The market is open Monday to Saturday, in the shadow of the impressive mid-20th-century city hall.

*From Norwich, follow signposts to the A47 east, which will take you direct to **Great Yarmouth**. **Caister-on-Sea** is a few miles to the north, along the A149.*

Drive north west on the A149 and west on the A1062 to Hoveton, where you need to turn left onto the A1151 to reach **Wroxham**. This route will take you past the Broads, but these are best explored by boat from **③** Wroxham.

Backtrack to Hoveton and turn west on the B1354 to reach the A140 north. From Aylsham, continue north on minor roads to reach **Blickling Hall**.

→ • • • • • • • • • ④

Clockwise from below:
Horsey Windpump, Norfolk Broads; Blickling Hall; Horatio Lord Nelson's school, North Walsham

2 GREAT YARMOUTH AND CAISTER-ON-SEA

Besides being a popular bucket-and-spade seaside resort complete with pier and a host of summer entertainments, **Great Yarmouth** was once one of Europe's main fishing ports, doing a roaring trade in kippers and bloaters. The **Time And Tide Museum of Great Yarmouth Life**, set in an old fish-curing factory, traces the town's fortunes, while the county's most famous seafarer, Horatio Lord Nelson, is remembered with an extensive collection of memorabilia at the **Norfolk Nelson Museum** on South Quay. There is also a Nelson memorial column at the southern end of the town.

Nearby **Caister-on-Sea**, another summer holiday town, has Roman remains including parts of a defensive wall, a gateway and remnants of other buildings, plus, just to the west, the impressive 27m-tall tower (90ft) of **Caister Castle**. Now largely in ruins, this romantic, moated, brick quadrangle fortress was built in 1432 by Sir John Falstaff, the rotund knight immortalised by Shakespeare in *Henry IV* and *The Merry Wives of Windsor*. Just to the north of Caister is the small settlement of **California**, which got its name at the time of the 19th-century American Gold Rush – possibly after some gold coins were unearthed here.

3 WROXHAM AND THE BROADS

The self-proclaimed 'Capital of the Broads', **Wroxham** is all about boating. It is a largely modern town with a bustling atmosphere (especially in high season), where shops and supermarket are geared to stocking up the fleets of Norfolk Broads hire boats – literally hundreds of vessels – that are headquartered here. Nevertheless, it is a pleasant spot to linger and watch the boats go by. There is also **Wroxham Barns**, a complex of tea-rooms, craftsmen's workshops, a junior farm and shops, to divert the attention.

If you prefer to be on the move, you will find plenty of guided waterborne tours as well as boats for daily hire. A famed holiday playground, the wondrous lakes and meres of the **Broads**, linked by pretty rivers, provide more than 125 miles of navigable waterways. Highlights are Barton Broad, where Nelson is said to have learned to sail, and Hickling Broad, which is impressive for its sheer size. Beware, however: the well-versed flock to watch novice boaters crunch their craft against the narrow spans of Potter Heigham Bridge, at the entrance to Hickling Broad. Even further east is Horsey Mere, popular with birdwatchers thanks to the **Horsey Mere Wildlife Reserve**. Nearby, the town of Horsey has a pretty little church with a Roman round tower, a 15th-century belfry and a picturesque thatched roof. The five-storey brick-built **Horsey Windpump** was once used to drain the surrounding countryside (which sits below sea level). It is now managed by the National Trust.

4 BLICKLING HALL

The first house to be built at Blickling belonged to Saxon King Harold until his death at the Battle of Hastings in 1066. Later, at the end of the 14th century, the land was redeveloped into a rectangular, moated mansion where Anne Boleyn is reputed to have been born – and although the house in which she probably spent much of her childhood is now gone, the present Blickling Hall is said to be haunted by her ghost. The red-brick house that stands here today, with its mullioned windows, profusion of towers and elegant gables, is a Jacobean creation – similar in design to Hatfield House *(see p41)*, which was built by the same architect. The house was requisitioned during World War II for use by the RAF, but has now been restored to its former glory by the National Trust. It is best known for its intricate plasterwork, its collection of more than 10,000 books, and its colourful formal gardens.

5 NORTH WALSHAM

Medieval Norfolk was a prosperous place thanks to the thriving wool trade, and many of the villages around North Walsham have surprisingly large and ornate churches as a result of that wealth. The town itself was a major weaving centre at that time, and it is now the largest town in North Norfolk. Centred around a busy and attractive market place and lots of shops – many of which are housed in attractive Georgian and Victorian buildings – North Walsham is probably most visited for its **Norfolk Motorcycle Museum**, which contains a large and fascinating collection of historic, mainly British, motorcycles and associated ephemera. North Walsham is also famous as the place where Horatio Nelson went to school, and you can still see his school building today.

Head east on minor roads, crossing the A140 and joining the B1145 near Banningham to continue east into **North Walsham**. ⑤

Instead of taking the direct route, turn off the A149 almost straight away and head north east to join the unclassified coast road at the little resort town of Mundesley. From here it is an 8-mile run north west into **Cromer**.

 • • • • • • • • • • ⑥

Clockwise from above:
the beach, Cromer; boat trip
to see the seals, Blakeney
Point; Sheringham Park;
windmill, Cley next the Sea

*Follow the A149 coast
road west all the way
to **Sheringham**.*

 7

6 CROMER

It is said that if you stand at the end of Cromer's little
pier, there is nothing between you and the North Pole
but sea – and this part of Norfolk is certainly an ideal
setting for bracing walks below the low cliffs. Once
a watering place for the well-heeled, Cromer became a
less exclusive resort town in the Victorian era when the
new railway brought the first flush of holidaymakers –
and it has changed very little since then. Besides the
usual seaside attractions, there is a splendid medieval
church, plus a pebble beach where semi-precious
amber and jet stone are often washed up. The town
is also known for the succulent crabs landed by its
fishing boats. The **RNLI Henry Blogg Museum**, with its
lifesaving displays, is named after the coxswain who
saved more than 800 lives at sea, only retiring in 1947
at the age of 71. Cromer hosts a popular carnival each
August and is backed by rolling woodland hills and
bracken-covered heath.

THE LOST VILLAGE OF SHIPDEN

Unlike the north norfolk coast further west,
which is slowly spreading out into the sea, the
coastline around Cromer is wracked by strong
tides and relentless erosion, and has been for
centuries. These days, there is a system of sea
defences in place to help protect the town,
but back in the 14th century a whole village
was swept away, and now lies several hundred
metres out to sea. The village of Shipden was
still standing, albeit underwater, in 1888 – when
an unlucky passenger steamer leaving Cromer
ran aground on its church spire.

7 SHERINGHAM

Today's Sheringham is a pleasingly genteel Victorian and Edwardian seaside resort. On a hill above it is Upper Sheringham, the original settlement. In the mid-1800s there was a busy fishing community here, with 150 working boats landing skate, cod, whiting, crabs and lobsters. It was not until the town was linked to the outside world by railway around the turn of the 20th century that Sheringham began absorbing the overspill holiday trade from neighbouring Cromer.

Like Cromer, Sheringham has an important lifeboat station, and there is information about the history of the town, including its lifeboats, in the **Sheringham Museum**. This is also a good spot to set off on the superb Peddars West and North Norfolk Coastal Path, which runs west all the way to Hunstanton. There are gardens to visit at **Sheringham Park** – a magnificent example of the 18th-century garden design work of Humphry Repton. Mature woodlands, rhododendrons, azaleas and rare shrubs are the stars of the show, while the viewing towers give amazing coastal vistas. Further west is the **Muckleburgh Collection**, the largest working military collection in private hands, which features 16 fully functioning tanks.

8 CLEY NEXT THE SEA

From Cley next the Sea, a four-mile-long spit of land known as **Blakeney Point** stretches out into the North Sea. Owned by the National Trust, it is popular with birdwatchers and is a delightful location for a nature walk. More than 300 different species of bird have been recorded just to the south on **Cley Marshes**, where a number of birdwatching hides have been constructed among the reed beds. Cley itself is an attractive little flintstone village that started out as a port on the once-navigable River Glaven – its large parish church is testimony to its former importance. Just to the west is the picturesque harbour town of **Blakeney**, where you can pick up a boat trip to see the seals on Blakeney Point. This is another good place to set off on a coastal walk – the whole North Norfolk coastline is designated an Area of Outstanding Natural Beauty.

Proceed along the A149 coast road to **Cley next the Sea**. 8

Continue along the A149 coast road through Morston and Stiffkey to reach **Wells-next-the-Sea**.
9

Clockwise from above:
Holkham Hall seen across the
gardens; interior of Holkham
Hall; sign for Wells-next-the-
Sea; the slipper chapel, Little
Walsingham; the beach at
Wells-next-the-Sea

9 WELLS-NEXT-THE-SEA

In Tudor times, Wells was right on the coast. Today it is one mile inland on an inlet that cuts through the reedbeds and marshes. The town – a pleasant mix of amusement arcades and curio shops, Georgian houses, pubs and teashops – is popular with yachtsmen and also has a small fishing fleet. One of its biggest landmarks, the huge granary building, has now been converted to luxury flats, but nevertheless features on many local postcards. However, by far Wells' biggest attraction is the huge expanse of flat sandy beach that stretches along the coast from just north of the town and can be reached by a pleasant walk through the pine woods.

Home to the Earl and Countess of Leicester, the vast 18th-century Palladian-style **Holkham Hall** sits at the centre of a massive 10,000-ha (25,000-acre) agricultural estate to the west of Wells. Besides guided tours of the state rooms, there is a bygones museum and a history of farming exhibition here, and you can also take electric launch trips on the vast formal lake. The house has a plethora of great paintings by the likes of Gainsborough, Poussin and Rubens on display, and there is also a connected gallery of contemporary art in the **Ancient House** in Holkham village.

NORFOLK'S STEAM RAILWAYS

Once one of the wealthiest and most populated places in England, Norfolk went into decline after the Black Death in the Middle Ages, and suffered centuries of isolation – until the arrival of the railways put the county back on the map. The great age of steam is celebrated across Norfolk today by a number of private rail companies run by groups of dedicated enthusiasts.

The **Wells and Walsingham Railway** runs a purpose-built Norfolk Hero steam locomotive from Wells-next-the-Sea to Little Walsingham, while the **Mid Norfolk Railway** operates between Dereham and Wymondham, in the heart of rural Norfolk. Further to the north east, the **Bure Valley Railway** offers trips from Aylsham to Wroxham, with the option of combining a train ride with a boat tour of the Broads. Finally, the main terminus of the five-mile-long **North Norfolk Railway** ('The Poppy Line') at Sheringham *(below)* has an interesting Museum Signal Box, while the same line's restoration works can be visited at Weybourne. The western terminus, near Holt, has a fascinating 28-sq-m model railway (300 sq ft). Most of Norfolk's steam railways are open through the summer period, with special events taking place on some lines in winter.

Take the B1105 south out of
Wells to Egmere, then turn
left onto the unclassified
road signposted for
Little Walsingham.

 ⑩

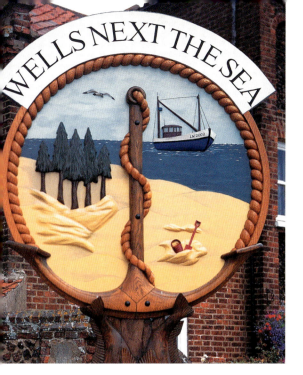

10　LITTLE WALSINGHAM

Set amid woodlands, Little Walsingham is a delightfully intact medieval village full of photogenic red-brick and half-timbered buildings. Its main street opens out into a square with a magnificent 16th-century octagonal pump-house. Little Walsingham became famous almost overnight in the 11th century, when a local lady, Richeldis de Faverches, is said to have been visited in several dreams by the Virgin Mary. She responded to these visions by building a reconstruction of Mary's home in Nazareth. This was a major destination for pilgrims between 1061, when the original **Shrine of Our Lady of Walsingham** was erected, and Henry VIII's Dissolution, when it was destroyed along with the Augustinian **Walsingham Priory**, whose atmospheric ruins still stand today. It was not until the early 20th century, when the **slipper chapel** (where the pilgrims traditionally left their shoes before walking the final mile to the shrine barefoot) was restored and an Anglican shrine added, that Walsingham regained its identity as a place of pilgrimage. Today, many thousands of pilgrims come here each year. The Georgian **Shirehall Museum** is set in an old courthouse near the abbey and has displays that chronicle Little Walsingham's history.

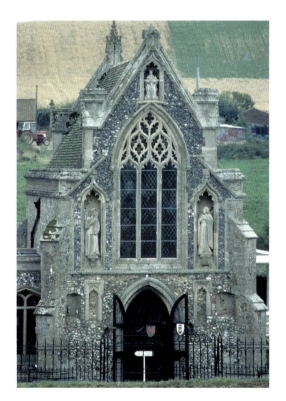

11　NORTH ELMHAM

The Saxon cathedral that once stood in the village of North Elmham was among the nation's earliest churches, and was once the seat of the Bishops of Norfolk. The ruins of the later **North Elmham Chapel** now stand on its site. An impressively large watermill also sits astride the River Wensum here. Four miles to the south, the **Norfolk Rural Life Museum**, near Gressenhall, has a wide range of exhibits on East Anglian country ways as they were in the past.

Head south on unclassified roads to Great and Little Snoring, crossing the A148 and bypassing Fakenham to join the A1067 south east. Turn right at Guist onto the B1110 and drive south to reach North Elmham. 11

Head east on the B1145 to join the A1067 for the run south east back to Norwich.

← • • • • • • • • • • 1

WITH MORE TIME

To the west of the tour, take time to visit the royal residence at Sandringham *(left)* and its 25ha (60 acres) of exotic gardens. It is from here that the Queen makes her annual Christmas broadcast to the nation. Just to the east is Houghton Hall, once the home of Britain's first prime minister, Sir Robert Walpole, while to the north is the pleasant little seaside resort of Hunstanton – which faces due west across The Wash to Lincolnshire, making for some stunning sunsets that mirror the colours in the layered cliffs.

Marshes and muses: nature and art along the Suffolk coast

Open heathland, secret woodlands and lonely marshes create an appropriately haunting ambience along Suffolk's vulnerable coast, which has fallen victim to repeated invasions over the centuries. More recently, the shingle beaches and backwater creeks – a familiar hangout of yachtsmen and fisherfolk – have inspired legions of artists and photographers, who never tire of the area's peculiarly East Anglian charm.

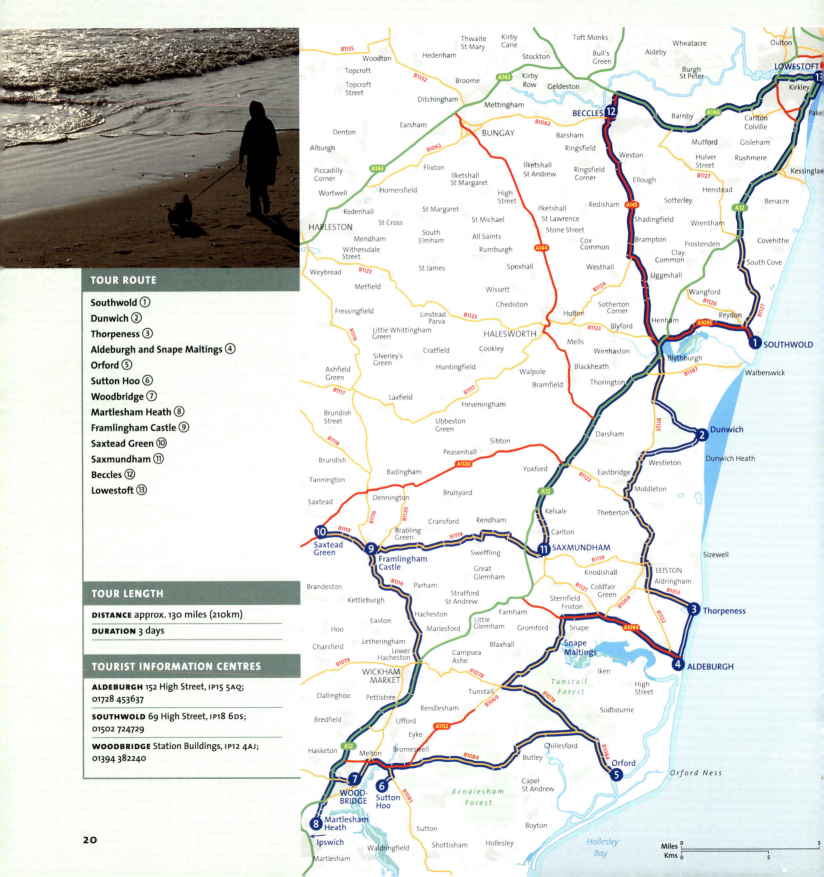

TOUR ROUTE

Southwold ①
Dunwich ②
Thorpeness ③
Aldeburgh and Snape Maltings ④
Orford ⑤
Sutton Hoo ⑥
Woodbridge ⑦
Martlesham Heath ⑧
Framlingham Castle ⑨
Saxtead Green ⑩
Saxmundham ⑪
Beccles ⑫
Lowestoft ⑬

TOUR LENGTH

DISTANCE approx. 130 miles (210km)

DURATION 3 days

TOURIST INFORMATION CENTRES

ALDEBURGH 152 High Street, IP15 5AQ;
01728 453637

SOUTHWOLD 69 High Street, IP18 6DS;
01502 724729

WOODBRIDGE Station Buildings, IP12 4AJ;
01394 382240

Clockwise from far left:
beach, Lowestoft; fishing
boats, Lowestoft; shop,
Southwold; Dunwich Heath;
Woodbridge Tide Mill

1 SOUTHWOLD

Claiming to be 'The Jewel of Suffolk', Southwold is
a classic East Anglian seaside town, and it's just as
appealing in the depths of winter as it is during high
season. There's a wealth of pretty Georgian architecture
around the central green, plus a host of small specialist
shops, a towering working lighthouse, the **Adnams
Brewery** with its renowned real ales, and, thanks to
some private enthusiasts, the first new pier to be built
in the UK since 1955. A row of aggressive-looking black
cannons pointing out to sea and an ornately fashioned
sign on the high street recall the great offshore battle
of Sole Bay, which, in 1672, saw off the Dutch and sealed
the supremacy of the Royal Navy. Also arranged in a
row, just below the cliffs, stand a collection of much-
photographed bathing huts that command prices that
would buy a nice semi-detached house elsewhere. Take
a boat trip on the *Coastal Voyager* if you want to see
the town from a different perspective, or cross the pretty
River Blyth on the pedestrian ferry to neighbouring
Walberswick, returning by the footbridge that uses
the trackbed of the long-defunct Southwold Railway.

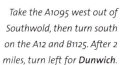

*Take the A1095 west out of
Southwold, then turn south
on the A12 and B1125. After 2
miles, turn left for **Dunwich**.* **2**

2 DUNWICH

Modern Dunwich, reached by a scenic drive through
pine woods and heathland, is a tiny and remote village
with a pleasant, nautically themed country pub. In the
Middle Ages, however, this was England's third most
important port after London and Bristol. While Bristol
lost its importance through silting up, the original city
of Dunwich suffered the opposite problem, falling
victim to the erosion that has been a perennial
problem along the east coast, and slowly crumbled
into the sea. Local folklore has it that on stormy
nights you can still hear the old church bells ringing
under water. This is now a nature conservation area
with a wealth of attractive coastal and woodland
walks – especially on **Westleton Heath** and the
National Trust's neighbouring **Dunwich Heath**.

*Take the unclassified road
to Westleton for the B1125
south. At the T-junction,
turn left onto the B1122 to
Aldringham, then turn
left onto the B1353 to
reach **Thorpeness**.*

Head south for 2 miles on the road beside the coastal dyke to reach Aldeburgh.

4

Drive west on the A1094 for 6 miles, then take the B1069 to Tunstall before turning left and crossing Tunstall Forest on the B1078 and B1084 to Orford.

5

Clockwise from below:
Snape Maltings; seafront buildings, Aldeburgh; Orford Castle

3 THORPENESS

This seaside village was created in the early 1900s when Scottish landowner and poet G Stuart Ogilvie bought the old fishing hamlet of Thorpe and proceeded to turn it into the idyllic little settlement we see today. To the north are low cliffs, while southwards stretches marshland that stands largely below sea level, protected by sea walls. Inland from the village is the picturesque **Meare**, a shallow, man-made lake whose tree-lined waters are home to a noisy congregation of waterfowl and sea birds, and are popular with boaters during the summer months.

Thorpeness's best-known landmark, however, is Ogilvie's remarkable **House in the Clouds** folly. Needing a 115,000-l (25,300-gallon) water tower to supply his newly built village, he disguised what would have been an eyesore by cladding it in wood to create living accommodation, and topping the structure with a two-storey clapboard 'house' (concealing the tank) that seems to be perched in the sky. Mary Mason, who lived in the house with her husband soon after it was built, wrote a series of popular children's poems here, one of which was inspired by her unusual home. Today, the house can be rented by holidaymakers. Nearby **Thorpeness Windmill** contains a helpful visitor centre.

4 ALDEBURGH AND SNAPE MALTINGS

Home to a thriving arts community and renowned for its eponymous music festival, the town of **Aldeburgh** is a pretty little place with galleries, antiques shops and restaurants lining a broad main street that runs parallel to the coast. Down on the shingle beach, fishermen still drag their boats ashore and sell their catch direct to the public – a scene that is very popular with photographers. The many historic buildings include the 16th-century Moot Hall, where council meetings are held to this day, and which also houses the small **Aldeburgh Museum**. Old maps show that the hall, now set on the seafront, was once considerably inland from a coast that has receded dramatically down the centuries. Aldeburgh is one of Europe's 20 nominated 'cultural villages' and hosts a colourful one-day carnival each August. It is also a popular sailing centre, and holds regattas in the summer months.

Six miles further inland, set beside the reed beds of the River Ore, the attractive complex of former Victorian industrial buildings at **Snape Maltings** was converted in 1967 into one of the nation's best-loved arts, culture and crafts centres, which includes a superb concert hall. Every June this highly atmospheric venue is the focus of the annual Aldeburgh Festival of Music and Arts.

5 ORFORD

The mighty keep of Orford's medieval **castle**, built by Henry II in 1165, stands as a reminder that this was once an important port. Now, though, it is a sleepy backwater full of pretty red-brick and half-timbered houses, and gastro pubs specialising in locally caught seafood. Reached by ferry, the long spit of land and shingle known as **Orford Ness** is home to a National Trust nature reserve. It was here that the inventor Barnes Wallace developed the bouncing bomb during World War II. It is possible to hike along the Ness all the way back to **Aldeburgh**.

6 SUTTON HOO

A hauntingly atmospheric site overlooking the tidal reaches of the peaceful River Deben, Sutton Hoo has not just one but a number of tumuli (burial mounds). For many visitors, however, the main attraction is the fascinating National Trust visitor centre. Displays here include a reconstruction of Sutton Hoo's most famous treasure, a Saxon burial ship that was excavated by dedicated local amateur archaeologist Basil Brown in 1939. The original items found in the ship, including gold jewellery and an iron-and-bronze helmet, are now on display in the British Museum, while at Sutton Hoo, there is an exhibition depicting how the Anglo-Saxon nobles lived and died, and how they founded their new kingdom of East Anglia. The shop has a first-rate selection of books on the area.

Follow the B1084 north and west, bearing left onto the A1152 and then turning left at the roundabout onto the B1083 to reach **Sutton Hoo** *after 1 mile.* 6

Backtrack to the A1152 and continue west to **Woodbridge***, following signs into the town centre.* 7

↓
*Head south on the
A12, following signs
to Martlesham and*
8 *Martlesham Heath.*

↓
*Backtrack to Woodbridge
and continue up the A12
to Lower Hacheston, where
you can pick up the B1116*
9 *to Framlingham Castle.*

↓
*Take the B1119 for a
short distance west to*
10 *reach Saxtead Green.*

*Return to Framlingham
and continue east on the
B1119, which leads you
right into Saxmundham.*

→ • • • • • • • • • • • **11**

7 WOODBRIDGE

Woodbridge is an attractive hilltop market town
dating back 1,500 years. It now has no fewer than
100 specialist shops, many on **The Thoroughfare**, a
classic English small-town high street. But much of
the town's appeal lies at a lower level, along the banks
of the lovely **River Deben**, with its bustling quayside.
The much-photographed 18th-century **tide mill** has
been restored to full working order and has some
interesting photographic and milling artefact displays.

8 MARTLESHAM HEATH

The World War II control tower at the old Martlesham
Heath airfield holds a **museum** dedicated to the
American bomber crews who flew from many local
air bases. Before the bombers arrived, Martlesham
Heath played a major role in the Battle of Britain.

9 FRAMLINGHAM CASTLE

One of Britain's largest and best preserved medieval
strongholds, mighty Framlingham Castle was a major
seat of Norman power from the 12th century. You can
walk the walls, explore the 13 great towers and the
outer courts, and wander by the moats and mere.
In turn a fortress, prison, poor house and school,
Framlingham is today an important reminder of our
nation's history. The adjacent town has many fine
buildings, some of which date back to Tudor times,
and some notable pubs. At nearby **Parham Airfield**,
the old control tower houses a museum to the American
390th Bomb Group, plus a fascinating display that
takes visitors through Winston Churchill's plans to set
up a resistance army in the event of a German invasion.

10 SAXTEAD GREEN

It's worth detouring slightly to Saxtead Green to visit
the **post mill**, a classic example of an East Suffolk-style
mill. Built in the 1300s, it has been the subject of
countless paintings and photos over the years. Climb
the stairs to see the machinery, which is all in full
working order – though it has not been in production
since 1947. The site is now cared for by English Heritage.

11 SAXMUNDHAM

A picturesque market town with a historic centre and many beautiful buildings, Saxmundham is a good place to stop for a quiet stroll. The local history society has published a **Town Trail**, which takes around an hour to walk and is a great way to acquaint yourself with the town's highlights – which include a typical Suffolk wool church and the remains of one of the tallest post mills in the county. There is also an interesting **museum** explaining the area's history.

12 BECCLES

Set beside the gentle **River Waveney**, which leads onto the renowned Norfolk Broads, this north Suffolk gem is the busiest market town in the district. Blessed with a profusion of fine Georgian, Regency and Victorian buildings, its conservation area centre is dominated by a lofty church tower. Host to a popular carnival and regatta each year, the town offers a pleasant **Marsh Trail** walk beside the river, while the open space of **Beccles Common** is a lovely setting for a leisurely picnic.

Clockwise from far left: the tide mill at Woodbridge; Saxtead Post Mill, Saxtead Green; Framlingham Castle

13 LOWESTOFT

Formerly one of England's leading fishing ports, Lowestoft now earns its keep by entertaining summer hordes with its sandy beaches, traditional seaside entertainments and pedestrianised shopping centre. The town's **Oulton Broad** and **Waveney River**, which offer guided boat tours, provide a gateway to a 125-mile, lock-free waterway system that straddles Suffolk and neighbouring Norfolk. A 1930s street scene is graphically re-created at the **East Anglia Transport Museum**, where steam, electric and motor vehicles are also on display and the tramway, trolley bus and narrow gauge steam railway can be ridden. The **Maritime Museum** recalls the era when the herring shoals yielded a rich harvest, with exhibits including models of historic and modern fishing vessels and an art gallery. Close by, **Africa Alive** has lions, giraffes, buffalo and hyenas wandering among 40ha (100 acres) of coastal parkland.

*Head north on the B1121 and pick up the A12 to Blythburgh, where you can turn onto the A145 to **Beccles**.* **12**

*Follow signs out of town for the A146 and drive east to reach **Lowestoft**.* **13**

*Follow the A12 south, turning left at Wrentham onto the B1127 to **Southwold**.* **1**

WITH MORE TIME

Despite being East Anglia's second city after Norwich, **Ipswich** is compact enough to enjoy an intimate, small-town atmosphere. The quayside on the River Orwell (from which George Orwell derived his sobriquet) has recently acquired an attractive cluster of plush modern apartments, trendy bars and eateries, but other parts of Ipswich are packed with history. Having reached the height of its power during the late 1500s, the town has a rich heritage of Elizabethan buildings, and the fine medieval churches and nearby Christchurch Mansion *(left)* are also worth a look.

Treasures of rural Suffolk

Timelessly English, inland Suffolk's rich, rolling countryside is dotted with fields of yellow rapeseed and golden wheat. Hedgerows teem with wildlife, rivers and streams flow gently through hidden valleys, and tiny villages full of half-timbered buildings and thatched cottages seem to appear at every turn in the road. Although this is not England's most dramatic scenery, the chalk downland in the east of the region makes it great horse country – and whether you're cantering cross-country or driving, you'll find the ambience is soft and languid in summer, yet somehow cosy and comforting in deepest winter.

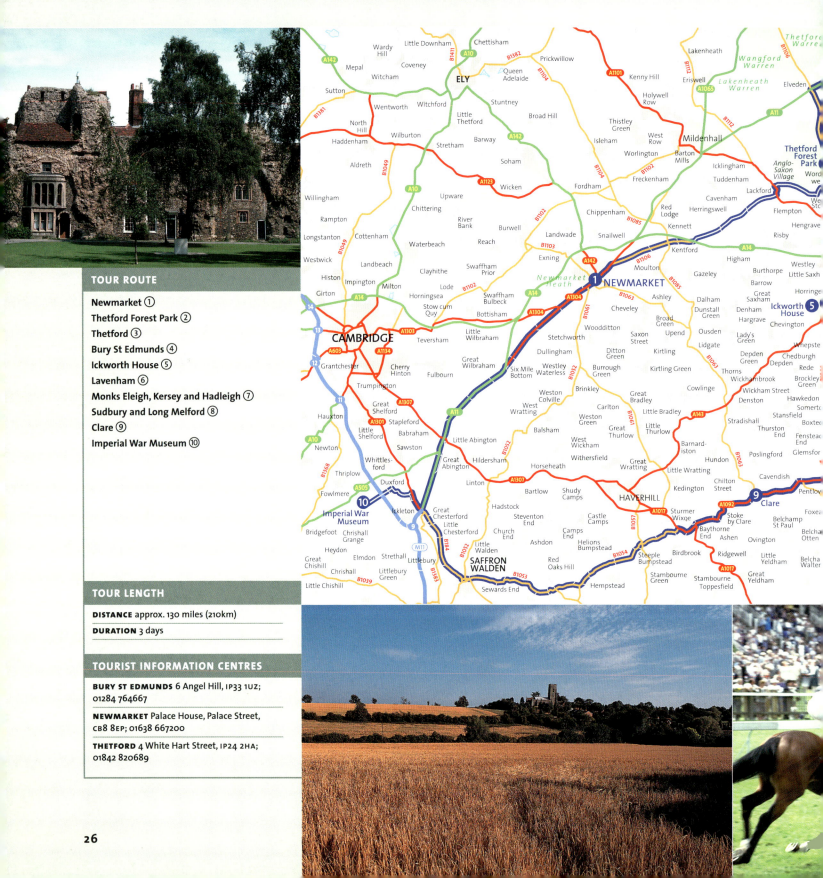

TOUR ROUTE

Newmarket ①
Thetford Forest Park ②
Thetford ③
Bury St Edmunds ④
Ickworth House ⑤
Lavenham ⑥
Monks Eleigh, Kersey and Hadleigh ⑦
Sudbury and Long Melford ⑧
Clare ⑨
Imperial War Museum ⑩

TOUR LENGTH

DISTANCE approx. 130 miles (210km)

DURATION 3 days

TOURIST INFORMATION CENTRES

BURY ST EDMUNDS 6 Angel Hill, IP33 1UZ; 01284 764667

NEWMARKET Palace House, Palace Street, CB8 8EP; 01638 667200

THETFORD 4 White Hart Street, IP24 2HA; 01842 820689

Clockwise from far left:
Bury St Edmunds;
half-timbered houses in
Lavenham; Newmarket
races; view over
cornfields to Kersey

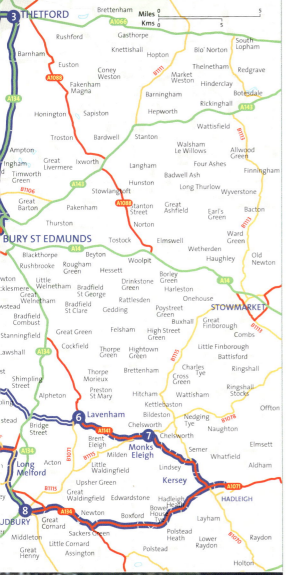

1 NEWMARKET

The town of Newmarket has been part of horse-racing history for more than 300 years: it was here, during the reign of Charles II, that the first horse race in Britain to be governed by written rules took place. The king held court here and even rode his own horse to racing victory, winning – as tradition dictates to this day – his weight in sausages. Today, Newmarket is the world's largest horse training centre – and a base for 2,500 racehorses, some 70 licensed trainers and 70 stud farms. Among them is **The National Stud**, which accommodates eight stallions and up to 200 mares, and offers visitors a rare chance to see behind the scenes of the equestrian world. Still on an equestrian theme, the **National Horseracing Museum** brings together such bizarre highlights as the stuffed head of Persimmon (winner of the 1896 Derby), the gun with which Victorian jockey Fred Archer committed suicide and the colourful jackets worn by Prince Monolulu, the eccentric 1950s tipster. Besides its two superb racecourses, Newmarket has a pretty town centre where you can buy, among other things, those famed local sausages.

*From Newmarket, take the A1304 north, forking right after 1 mile onto the B1506. Cross the A14 and continue north east on unclassified roads to Lackford, then on to West Stow and the entrance to **Thetford Forest Park**'s southern section.* 2

2 THETFORD FOREST PARK

A patchwork of heath and pine and broadleaf woodland, this area of delightfully undeveloped countryside was designated a forest park in 1990 and now attracts 1.5 million visitors each year. The lovely seasonal colours make it a magical place for a stroll, with abundant wildlife and rare plants throughout the forest, plus more than 200 species of tree from around the world at **Lynford Arboretum**. There are also archaeological and historical sites such as **Grimes Graves** *(see p28)* and, in the southern part of the forest (also known as **West Stow Country Park**), a reconstructed **Anglo-Saxon Village** features full-size replicas of houses similar to those that stood on the site in the Dark Ages.

*Take the B1106 north to join the A11, turn right to pass through Elvedon and enter **Thetford** after 4 miles.*
 3

Clockwise from above:
Tudor chimneys and the
cathedral, Bury St Edmunds;
the abbey, Bury St Edmunds;
Ickworth House; the Nutshell,
Bury St Edmunds

3 THETFORD

Although modern Thetford may seem unremarkable at
first glance, this is a place rich in history and teeming
with archaeological sites. A town was already established
here on the ancient Icknield Way when the flint mines
at **Grimes Graves** first came into use around 2500BC.
Some 2,000 years later, the Celtic Iceni tribe built
earthwork fortifications – parts of which survive –
to defend this strategically placed settlement. Despite
this they later became vassals of the Romans, prompting
the famous uprising by their warrior queen Boudicca.
Under King Canute's rule, Thetford was prosperous
enough to have its own mint, and by the time of the
Norman Conquest in 1066, this was England's sixth
largest town, with a population of around 4,000.

Thetford grew again under the Normans, gaining
a castle, a cathedral and a priory. The atmospheric
ruins of **Thetford Priory**, dissolved during the 16th
century by Henry VIII, stand on the north bank of the
river, while an impressively large **castle mound** still
dominates the landscape to the east of the town.
Although nothing remains of the cathedral, Thetford
retains a bishop to this day.

GRIMES GRAVES

Using antlers as picks and animals' shoulder
bones as shovels, Neolithic workers at Grimes
Graves, six miles north west of Thetford, sank
more than 350 mine shafts up to 9m (30ft)
deep to extract highly prized flint for trading.
Archaeologists found one antler still bearing
the imprint of a miner's finger, intact after
more than 4,000 years. Today, visitors can
descend a shaft to view seven radiating galleries,
and in summer there are also demonstrations
of flint-knapping – the technique for shaping
flint into tools such as axe heads.

*Follow the A134 south
for some 12 miles into
Bury St Edmunds.*

 4

4 BURY ST EDMUNDS

Tied to a tree and shot full of arrows by invading Danes, the martyred Saxon King Edmund was England's patron saint until the Normans eventually replaced him with St George. The mighty **St Edmundsbury Abbey**, built with stone shipped in from Caen in France, grew up around his shrine and came to be England's most important pilgrimage site after Canterbury. The abbey was razed during Henry VIII's dissolution of the monasteries, but haunting ruins remain within the delightful gardens.

Adjacent to the abbey ruins is the former church of St James, converted to an Anglican **cathedral** in 1914 and rejuvenated in the second half of the 20th century by the remarkable Stephen Dykes Bowers, who started out as the architect and ended up funding the multi-million-pound project out of his own pocket. His crowning legacy is the wonderful mock-Gothic tower, completed in 2004.

The bustling market town of Bury St Edmunds, which grew up around the abbey, has half-a-dozen more fine churches and an impressive market with a glorious **Corn Exchange**. This now houses shops and cafes, the delightful Georgian **Theatre Royal**, and **Moyse's Hall Museum** with its grizzly artefacts from the notorious Red Barn murders of 1827. Not to be missed is the **Manor House Museum**, housing the Allen Collection of American Clocks and the Irene Barnes Collection of 1920s and 1930s dresses. An attraction of a different kind, the **Nutshell** claims to be Britain's smallest pub – eight is a crowd!

5 ICKWORTH HOUSE

The dramatic central rotunda and gracefully curving wings of Ickworth House were designed in 1795 for the eccentric Frederick Hervey, fourth Earl of Bristol and Bishop of Derry, to house his collections. The magnificent state rooms display Georgian silver, Regency furniture and the works of old masters such as Titian, Velasquez and Gainsborough. The building's stunning grounds comprise 730ha (1,800 acres) of beautiful parkland, partly laid out by 'Capability' Brown and with formal Italian-style and rose gardens created by the First Marquess of Bristol in the Victorian era.

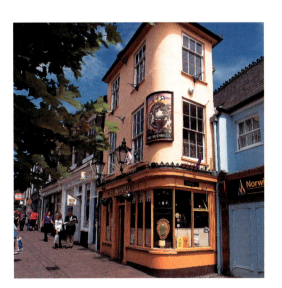

Take the A143 south west of Bury to the village of Horringer and Ickworth House. **5**

Backtrack a little on the A143 before turning right onto the B1066. From Hartest, follow signs to Lavenham.

6

Clockwise from above:
Kersey; Kentwell House, Long Melford; aircraft at the Imperial War Museum; church, Long Melford

*Follow the A1141 south east through **Monks Eleigh** and on towards Hadleigh. **Kersey** is signposted to the right just before you reach **Hadleigh**.*

⑦

*Take the A1071 west, then turn right onto the A134 to reach **Sudbury**. **Long Melford** is 4 miles further north, on the B1064.*

→ • • • • • • • ⑧

6 LAVENHAM

Often described as the most complete medieval town in Britain – and certainly one of the most photographed – Lavenham is full of half-timbered and plaster houses, with bleached wood and whitewash contrasting vividly with hues of pastel pink. The glorious **guildhall** houses a permanent local history exhibition, while the **Wool Hall** bears testament to the source of the town's enormous wealth in the Middle Ages. There's also an outstanding market cross and the grand **St Peter and St Paul church**, where highlights range from the massive 43m-tall tower (141ft) to the humorous 15th-century carvings on the miserichord – including one of a man squeezing a pig to make it squeal. Lavenham has featured in numerous movies and TV shows, from *The Canterbury Tales* to *Witchfinder General*, *The 13 Chairs*, *Barry Lyndon* and *Lovejoy*, and each August the town hosts around 250 rare and exotic vehicles at its Rare Breeds Motor Show.

7 MONKS ELEIGH, KERSEY AND HADLEIGH

These three classic 'Constable Country' villages are set close together in the River Brett valley. **Monks Eleigh**'s superb St Peter's church is set at the end of a row of lime trees and is visible for miles around, while **Kersey**, one of Suffolk's prettiest little hidden villages, is tucked away in the lanes. Here, ancient cottages cluster around a picturesque ford, and it sometimes seems as though time has stood still for hundreds of years. Kersey cloth made the village extremely prosperous in medieval times and it still exudes a well-contented air today. Stop to look in the main street in **Hadleigh** and you'll find any number of postcards and prints depicting the local St Mary's church. Constable, Gainsborough, Turner and Morris all produced paintings of this elegant place of worship. Close by are the pretty half-timbered medieval and Victorian **guildhall** complex and the 1595 red-brick **Deanery**, with its imposing polygonal twin turrets.

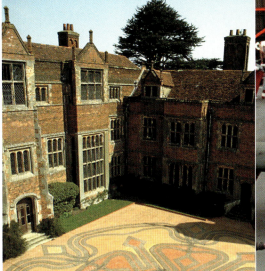

9 CLARE

A pleasant small town on the River Stour, Clare has an impressive church dating mostly from the 15th century, an old market square and a bevy of antiques shops and galleries. To the south of the town, the site of **Clare Castle** has been altered over the years, and Clare's original railway station (now no longer in use) stands within the castle walls. Nevertheless, significant earthworks remain – including a high castle mound with pretty views over the town, plus the ruin of the stone keep. The castle is now surrounded by a **country park**, which has a helpful visitor centre and offers walks along the old railway line.

 Follow the A1092 west from Long Melford to reach **Clare**. 9

10 IMPERIAL WAR MUSEUM

A World War I and II heritage site, the Imperial War Museum at Duxford is recognised as Europe's premier aviation museum, as well as having a vast collection of tanks, military vehicles and naval exhibits. On the same site, the American Air Museum in Britain stands as a memorial to the 30,000 British-based American flyers who lost their lives in World War II. The impressive collection, which includes a B17 Flying Fortress, is housed in a striking glass-fronted building. Duxford regularly hosts air shows and, as of summer 2006, AirSpace, a display of 30 rare and historic British and Commonwealth aircraft – both military and civilian.

Continue west on the A1092, A1017, B1054 and B1053 to Saffron Walden. From there, take the B184 north to Great Chesterford, cross the roundabout to join the A1301, and follow the signs for the **Imperial War Museum**. 10

Backtrack to the A11 north, forking right after 7 miles onto the A1304. Follow this road through Six Mile Bottom to **Newmarket**.

8 SUDBURY AND LONG MELFORD

In the busy Suffolk market town of **Sudbury**, you can visit **Gainsborough's House**, where the painter was born; take a tour round **Vanners**, a working silk mill; or cruise the Stour aboard a Victorian launch. In the heart of the Stour Valley, **Long Melford** is renowned for its antiques shops, the imposing Tudor mansion **Melford Hall** and a magnificent **church**. Half a mile north is **Kentwell Hall**, a romantic moated Tudor manor in lovely gardens. Attractions include historic farm buildings with rare breed animals, hugely popular open-air plays and concerts (for which pre-booking is essential) and re-creations of Tudor life, during which up to 250 men, women and children dress and act as their Elizabethan ancestors would have done.

WITH MORE TIME

A prominent wool trade town during the 17th and 18th centuries, **Stowmarket** is still an important local hub today, and it makes an appropriate location for the splendid **Museum of East Anglian Life** *(left)*. Set in 28ha (70 acres), this venue has more than enough variety to fill an afternoon – from Suffolk Punch horses and steam engines to a smithy, a watermill and a collection of reconstructed rural buildings. Nearby is the Redwings Horse Sanctuary, which provides a home for unwanted horses, ponies and donkeys, and has a busy programme of events in the summer months.

The pleasant charms of Essex

Essex is one of England's best-kept secrets. Too many people form their opinion from travelling the county's frenetic motorways and trunk roads, but dive off into the web of country lanes and you will find a wholly different world. Here are some of our prettiest small towns and villages, where clapboard vies with half-timbering, and warm red brick with brightly painted plasterwork. Here too are splendid castles and majestic stately homes – and a wonderful coastline that contrasts traditional bustling seaside resorts with lonely marshes and expansive salt flats.

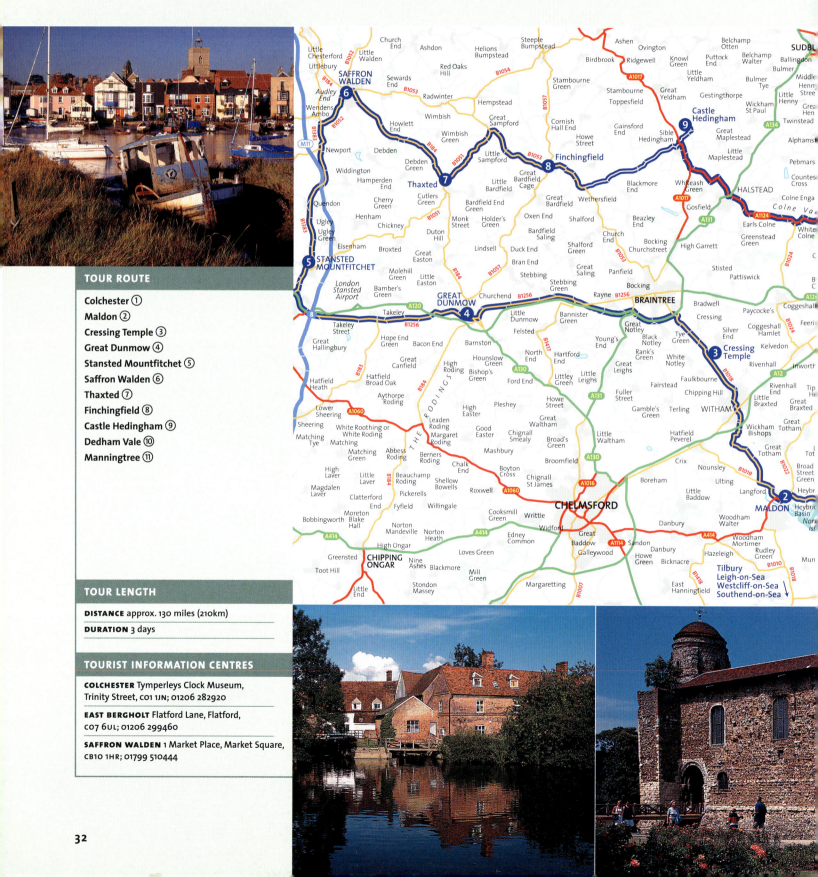

TOUR ROUTE

Colchester ①
Maldon ②
Cressing Temple ③
Great Dunmow ④
Stansted Mountfitchet ⑤
Saffron Walden ⑥
Thaxted ⑦
Finchingfield ⑧
Castle Hedingham ⑨
Dedham Vale ⑩
Manningtree ⑪

TOUR LENGTH

DISTANCE approx. 130 miles (210km)

DURATION 3 days

TOURIST INFORMATION CENTRES

COLCHESTER Tymperleys Clock Museum, Trinity Street, CO1 1JN; 01206 282920

EAST BERGHOLT Flatford Lane, Flatford, CO7 6UL; 01206 299460

SAFFRON WALDEN 1 Market Place, Market Square, CB10 1HR; 01799 510444

Clockwise from far left:
River Colne, near Colchester;
timber-framed buildings,
Colchester; art exhibit
at firstsite, Colchester;
Colchester Castle;
Dedham, Dedham Vale

1 COLCHESTER

In Roman times, Camulodunum, as Colchester was originally called, was the capital of Britain and the nation's earliest recorded town. Today, it does not even rate as the county town of Essex – that's Chelmsford – but, snug within its substantially complete city walls, it remains a vibrant centre of entertainment, commerce and good living. Here, you will find **Colchester Castle**, Europe's largest Norman keep, within which is a fascinating local history museum. Currently housed just opposite in the Georgian Minories building, the **firstsite** art gallery is a must for anyone with an interest in contemporary art and design. The **Dutch Quarter** is full of picturesque little streets, and **Castle Park** is a traditional Victorian splash of green enlivened with vivid colour from inventive floral displays. The adjacent **Hollytrees Museum** is an attractive Georgian townhouse museum, while **Tymperleys Clock Museum** occupies a 15th-century former residence and contains a specialist collection of timepieces – all of which were made in the town. Set in 25 beautiful hectares (60 acres), **Colchester Zoo** claims to be Britain's fastest-growing animal park. Here, you can see more than 200 different species, including lions, giraffes, zebras, elephants, rhinos and pygmy hippos. Some £2 million has been invested in the Play Patagonia sea lion underwater experience, and other key attractions include penguin parades and falconry displays. Offering a slower pace of life, **High Woods Country Park** was once a royal hunting forest and today provides 135ha (330 acres) of recreational land, including nature trails and guided walks.

*Leave Colchester on the B1025 heading south. After 4 miles, fork right at Abberton, passing the reservoir on an unclassified lane. At the B1026, turn left to reach **Maldon**.*

Clockwise from above:
Maldon; Audley End,
near Saffron Walden; the
Lawrence Washington
window, Purleigh
church, Maldon

2 MALDON

Heading south from Colchester, the route takes you past
the road to **Mersea Island**, the most easterly of the British
Isles. Take the causeway across to see the oyster beds
where the renowned Colchester natives – reputedly the
world's finest – are raised. Maldon is an attractive town
overlooking marshes, the Blackwater estuary and Norsey –
the island where Saxons and Danes fought a ferocious
battle. The town's many fine buildings include the 16th-
century Moot Hall and 17th-century Dr Plume's Library.
Historic Thames sailing barges, with their distinctive
rust-coloured sails, can often be seen tied up at Hythe
Wharf, beside the pleasant waterfront **Promenade Park**.
Sea salt has been produced in Maldon since 1882.

A few miles to the south, **Purleigh church** is worth
a short detour to look at the stained-glass window
commemorating Lawrence Washington – a former
rector of Purleigh and the great-great-grandfather
of the first US president, George Washington.

*Take the B1019 and then
the B1018 north through
Witham to reach
Cressing Temple.*

 • • • • • • • • • • ③

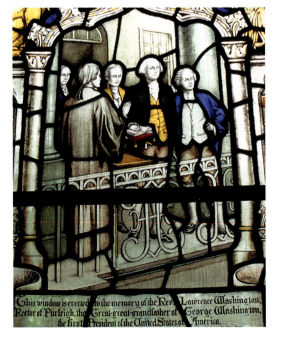

34

3 CRESSING TEMPLE

The name is rather misleading as this is not the site of any place of worship, but rather the location of two incredible secular structures; vast medieval barns that once belonged to the Knights Templar religious order. Cathedral-like in their proportions, the barns are thought to be the best-preserved examples of 13th-century timber-framed barns in Europe. Also here is a re-created Tudor garden, including a potager and a knot garden.

4 GREAT DUNMOW

Strung along one main road, Great Dunmow is a pleasant small town with some nice Victorian, Regency, Georgian and earlier buildings. It is best known for the quirky **Dunmow Flitch Trials**, a ceremony dating from the 12th century in which a side of bacon is presented to any husband and wife who can prove that they have gone a whole year without domestic dispute! The trials take place every four years; the next occurence will be in July 2008. Great Dunmow is also a gateway to the **Rodings**, a collection of tiny but delightful villages strung along the unspoilt valley of the River Roding.

5 STANSTED MOUNTFITCHET

The modern, Richard Rogers-designed building and busy runways of London Stansted Airport may be just across the motorway, but you can step right back in time at **Mountfitchet Castle.** The motte-and-bailey castle and adjacent village have been reconstructed on their original site to give a vivid glimpse of what life was like in Norman times. Houses, a church, a siege tower, costumed figures and a programme of events bring the Domesday Book era vividly to life. On the village's attractive main street stands the **House on the Hill Museum Adventure**. Embark on a nostalgia trip and rediscover your favourite teddy bear, Action Man, Sindy, Barbie and Ken at this wonderful toy museum set on two capacious floors. Besides 19th- and 20th-century toys, there are collections of seaside slot machines and theatre, film and TV memorabilia.

6 SAFFRON WALDEN

The once super-wealthy town of Walden made its fortune from crops grown on the fertile land that surrounded it. One of these was the crocus flower from which saffron is processed and which gave the town its present name. That trade had largely disappeared by the 1700s, but the town retains a profusion of fine buildings dating from the Middle Ages and is a joy to visit. In addition, there's a vast Gothic church, a ruined keep and a mile-long turf maze. The major local attraction, however, is **Audley End**, one of England's greatest Jacobean houses, set in a 'Capability' Brown landscape with a delightful walled kitchen garden. James I once described Audley End as: 'Too big for a King' as it was the largest house in existence when built in 1614. However, by 1750, two thirds of the building had been demolished. Today, some 31 rooms – many of them modelled by Robert Adam – can be visited for an evocative taste of how the great and the good used to live.

*Continue on the B1018 to the A120. Turn left and then turn off at the B1256 to reach **Great Dunmow**.* ④

*Head west on the B1256. Cross the M11 onto the A120 and, shortly after, turn right on the B1383 following signs for **Stansted Mountfitchet**.* ⑤

*Continue north on the B1383 until you reach the B1052. Turn right to reach **Saffron Walden**. Shortly before the town is a sign to the left for Audley End.* ⑥

*Head south east on the B184 until you arrive at **Thaxted**.* ⑦

Clockwise from above:
Thaxted Church, Thaxted;
Willy Lott's cottage, Dedham;
river at Manningtree; village
of Finchingfield

7 THAXTED

Set amid the rolling North Essex uplands, Thaxted's imposing Norman **church** has a tower that soars a giddying 55m (181ft). The 1804-built **John Webb's Windmill** and the town's collection of gorgeous, rickety-looking, half-timbered buildings, including a pretty market hall, make this one of the county's most photographed places. Thaxted's medieval prosperity came from the cutlery trade, and it was the Guild of Cutlers that built the striking **guildhall**, which has been beautifully restored.

8 FINCHINGFIELD

Delightful Finchingfield, set on a hill that rises above its village green and large duckpond, stars on countless calendars and regularly vies with Castle Coombe, in Wiltshire, for the title of 'England's prettiest village'. There is a neat town church with a squat clocktower, and also an attractive 16th-century guildhall and an 18th-century Dutch windmill. Look out for examples of pargeting (decorative plasterwork) on village buildings – this tradition is common to the area.

⊕ *Double back on the B184*
until you reach the B1051.
Follow the road to the
B1053 and turn right to
⑧ *Finchingfield*.

Continue on the B1053
until Wethersfield. Here,
take the unclassified road
north to Sible Hedingham.
Cross the A1017 and
take the minor road to
Castle Hedingham.

→ • • • • • • • • • • • ⑨

9 CASTLE HEDINGHAM

The village of Castle Hedingham's crowning glory is its mighty Norman keep. This is all that remains of **Hedingham Castle**, built in 1140 by Aubrey de Vere, but it is widely considered England's finest keep, and the impressive banqueting hall inside is spanned by the largest Norman arch in Europe. Jousts and other events are held in the summer, but even without these added draws it is a more than worthwhile attraction. Also in the village is **St Nicholas Church**, which dates from the same period and has an unusual Norman Wheel Window with stained glass, attractive carved miserichords and three beautiful original doors. Just outside the village is the **Colne Valley Railway**, a one-mile stretch of heritage track where visitors can ride on – and even drive – a variety of vintage steam locomotives.

10 DEDHAM VALE

The country idyll of John Constable's work springs back to life in the peaceful valley of the River Stour and in the villages of **Dedham**, **Flatford** and, just across the Suffolk border, **East Bergholt** – where the artist was born. Arts courses are now taught in **Flatford Mill**, a subject favoured by the great man. Willy Lott's cottage is another landmark that features in several of Contstable's paintings but is not open to the public. Just upstream, **Bridge Cottage** contains an exhibition on the artist.

11 MANNINGTREE

The estuary town of Manningtree has fine Georgian buildings and a pleasant riverside promenade. It is a yachtsman's haven, known for its flock of swans that sedately patrol the River Stour. On the hill above is the adjacent small town of **Mistley**. Here, imposing gatehouse lodges and two square towers topped with domes are all that remain of the great house and church designed and built by Robert Adam in 1782.

Return to the A1017 and head south. Fork off to the left on the A1124, then turn left onto the A12 and take the third turning past junction 29 to reach Dedham and **Dedham Vale**. 🔟

Take unclassified roads south to the A137 where you turn left for **Manningtree**. ⑪

Return to **Colchester** *on the A137.*
← • • • • • • • • • • • ❶

WITH MORE TIME

Along the Thames Estuary, **Tilbury** has an impressive 17th-century fort, built in response to Dutch incursions and which saw active service during both world wars. Overlooking Canvey Island, **Leigh-on-Sea** has quaint clapboard houses and is known for its cockles and whelks. For other tastes, one of life's great pleasures is a Rossi ice cream consumed while strolling the seafront that runs between **Westcliff-on-Sea** and neighbouring **Southend-on-Sea** *(left)*. The latter's pier is the longest in the world and contributes to the resort's enduring popularity.

Hertfordshire's houses and gardens

Green and leafy Hertfordshire is one of England's smaller counties: a pleasant and prosperous place bejewelled with historic stately homes and impressive Roman remains. In spite of its proximity to London – and the many commuters who live here – this is still essentially a region characterised by fields and hedgerows, pretty villages and networks of narrow, winding country lanes. Rapeseed has replaced the traditional wheat, oats and barley as the predominant crop, but the fields are still a blaze of colour come harvest time – though it's now brilliant yellow rather than gold.

TOUR ROUTE

St Albans ①

Gardens of the Rose ②

Hatfield and Welwyn Garden City ③

Knebworth House ④

Benington ⑤

Hertford ⑥

Henry Moore Foundation ⑦

Royston ⑧

Baldock and Hitchin ⑨

Shaw's Corner ⑩

TOUR LENGTH

DISTANCE approx. 95 miles (150km)

DURATION 3 days

TOURIST INFORMATION CENTRES

HERTFORD 10 Market Place, SG14 1DF; 01992 584322

LUTON Luton Central Library, St George's Square, LU1 2NG; 01582 401579

ST ALBANS Town Hall, Market Place, AL3 5DJ; 01727 864511

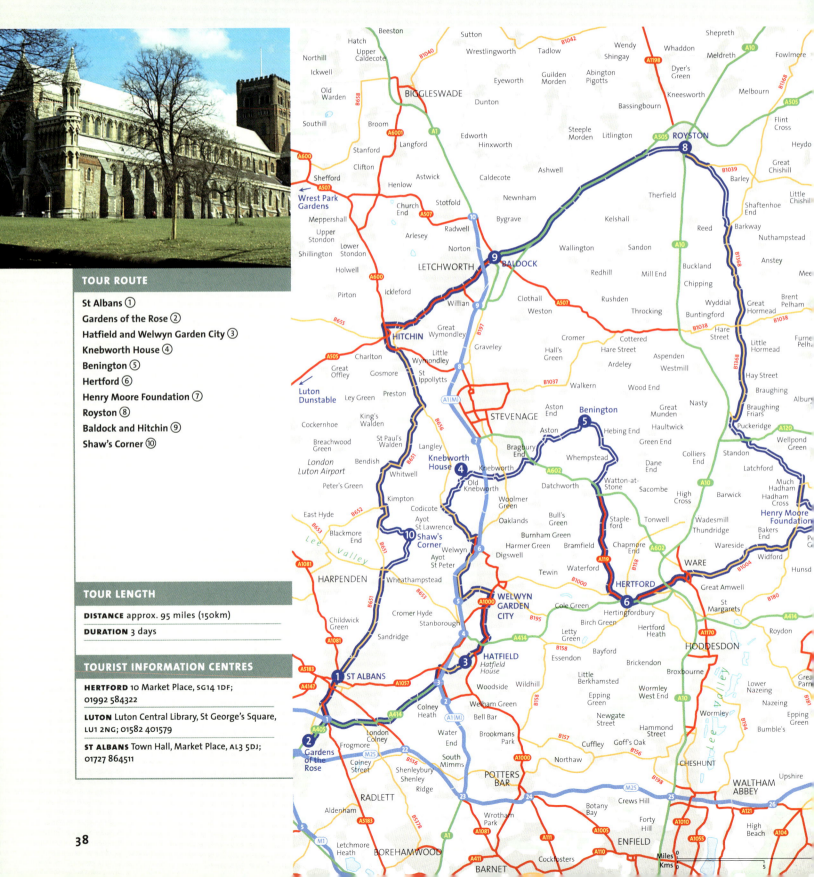

Standing on the ruins of Verulamium, the third largest city in Roman Britain, St Albans is an attractive place with a steep, picturesque high street, a bustling market-town atmosphere and a pretty jumble of architectural styles. Built around the truly magnificent **Cathedral and Abbey Church of St Alban**, the city takes its name from Britain's first Christian martyr, a soldier of Verulamium who lost his head in AD250 for sheltering a priest. St Albans Abbey, as the cathedral is known locally, belonged to a former Benedictine monastery, founded in 1077 on the execution site. Its impressive tower contains bricks salvaged from the (by then abandoned) Roman city, and elements of a Saxon monastic building constructed in the 8th century by King Offa of Mercia can also be seen. Inside the cathedral is a shrine to St Alban, plus many exceptional wall paintings and an interesting multimedia show. Just to the west, the former abbey gateway is now occupied by St Albans School, one of whose early students was Nicholas Breakspear, who in the 12th century became England's only pope.

Just to the north of the abbey site, St Albans' **medieval clocktower** with its mighty Gabriel bell – which actually predates the building – is one of only two of its kind in the country. Probably built by the townspeople as an assertion of their independence from the abbey, the tower is still a major landmark. You can climb to the top for sweeping views over the surrounding countryside. The story of the city from the end of the Roman era to the present day is related at the nearby **Museum of St Albans**, which also features a pleasant wildlife garden.

Among the impressive ruins of Verulamium to the west of the modern city centre is a **Roman Theatre** discovered in 1847 and excavated in 1935. Believed to have been built around AD160, this semi-circular structure would have held up to 2,000 spectators. In **Verulamium Park** are the remains of a Roman bathhouse, a basilica and part of the city wall, as well as the Verulamium Museum, which features some wonderful Roman mosaics, reconstructed rooms, discovery areas and interactive displays providing a very real insight into everyday life in Roman Britain.

Clockwise from far left: St Albans Abbey; Standon, near the Henry Moore Foundation; detail of St Albans Abbey; St Albans

From St Albans, head for the A405 south and then follow signs to Chiswell Green and the Gardens of the Rose.

Clockwise from above:
Gardens of the Rose; interior
at Hatfield House; the house
and gardens at Hatfield;
Brocket Hall; detail of roses

2 GARDENS OF THE ROSE

Run by the Royal National Rose Society, the spectacular
5-ha (12 acre) Gardens of the Rose in Chiswell Green
showcase an incredible 1,600 varieties of this most
popular of garden plants, ranging from time-honoured
favourites to the latest experimental hybrids. With
more than 30,000 specimens, this is said to be the
largest collection of its kind in the world, and during
the summer months the beautiful fragrance can be
almost overwhelming.

FLYING HIGH

Hertfordshire has had links with aviation since
1784, when the first hot air balloon flight over
Britain landed at Standon Green End. In the 20th
century, de Havilland developed a formidable
reputation for its aircraft, which were produced
at a base in Hatfield. The aircraft are now made
in Canada, but the de Havilland Aircraft Heritage
Centre at London Colney recalls the early days
of one of aviation's greatest names. More than
20 aircraft types, both military and commercial,
are on display – including the prototype of the
famed Mosquito fighter-bomber, the Tiger
Moth biplane in which so many learned to fly,
and the Vampire and Venom jet fighters.

*Backtrack to the main road
and drive north east on the
A405 and A414 to reach
Hatfield. Continue east
through the town to reach
Hatfield House, from where
it is a 2-mile drive north up
the A1000 to **Welwyn**.*

3   HATFIELD AND WELWYN GARDEN CITY

The future Elizabeth I – 'Good Queen Bess' – spent her early years at **Hatfield**, and one wing of her childhood home, now known as the Old Palace, still stands in the grounds of the magnificent **Hatfield House**. The land was acquired soon after Elizabeth's death by Robert Cecil, first Earl of Salisbury and principal secretary of state to both the queen and her successor, James I. He demolished the majority of the palace, replacing it with the fine country house that has been home to the Cecil family ever since. One of the nation's most outstanding Jacobean mansions, this gracious building is jam-packed with armour, fine furniture, tapestries and works of art, and also features a collection of Queen Elizabeth's personal possessions, which have been acquired by the family over the years. In the 17-ha (42-acre) great park are some pleasant formal gardens, a knot garden and a scented garden, plus woodlands, nature trails and a beautiful lake.

Though it is located just off the busy A1(M), **Welwyn Garden City** is a pleasant backwater, and worth a stop to visit the interesting **Mill Green Museum**. The 18th-century watermill here is in full working order, and now houses an interesting collection of historical artefacts. Also close by is **Brocket Hall**, a beautiful stately home that has now been converted to a hotel. Its titled former owner earned himself a prison term when, strapped for cash, he apparently pushed his collection of rare Ferrari cars into the lake and tried to claim the insurance money.

HERTFORDSHIRE'S GARDEN CITIES

A 20th-century experiment in town planning, Hertfordshire's garden cities were created by Ebenezer Howard, who objected to the poor working and living conditions in Britain's industrial cities and dreamed of combining 'the health of the country with the comfort of the town'. Begun in 1903, Letchworth was the first of the garden cities, and Welwyn followed soon afterwards. The fruits of Howard's vision – towns made up of broad, tree-lined avenues and surrounded by open countryside – are still visible here today.

Head west from the town centre to pick up the B197 north. After crossing the A1(M), continue on the B656 and follow signs for **Knebworth House**.

Clockwise from above:
Knebworth House and
gardens; Sheep Piece 1971–72,
Henry Moore Foundation;
field of poppies near Baldock

*Follow unclassified lanes
east via Knebworth and
⑤ Aston to reach **Benington**.*

*Head south on minor roads
via Watton-at-Stone to join
⑥ the A119 into **Hertford**.*

*Take the A119 east to
Ware then join the B1004
through Wareside. From
Widford, continue east
on unclassified roads
to Perry Green and the
⑦ Henry Moore Foundation.*

*Head north west via Much
Hadham and Puckeridge to
the B1368. Continue north
on this road to Barkway,
then turn left onto the
unclassified road to **Royston**.*

⑧

4 KNEBWORTH HOUSE

In recent years, the expansive grounds of Knebworth
House have played host to many major rock music
concerts. At other times, the 100-ha (250-acre) deer park
is the epitome of peace and quiet. Home to the Lytton
family since 1490, the house itself features an eclectic
mix of decorative styles from the last 500 years, while
the gardens were an inspired collaborative creation
of the great early-20th-century architect Sir Edwin
Lutyens and gardening genius Gertrude Jekyll.

5 BENINGTON

A little way further along the route to the east, the
picturesque village of Benington is a traditional-
looking place centred around a village green. It is worth
stopping here to see the lovely **Benington Lordship
Gardens**. The colourful seasonal floral displays range
from snowdrops in winter to roses in summer.

6 HERTFORD

Hertfordshire's county town has numerous worthy
old buildings. **Hertford Castle** was in its day a favoured
royal residence, where Henry VI spent much of his
childhood – as did the three children of Henry VIII. All
that remains of the castle today is its gatehouse, and
although this is now given over to offices, tours can be
arranged. Running through Hertford is the lovely River
Lea, which for much of its route down to London runs
parallel to the **Lea Navigation Canal**, a waterway that
is popular with leisure boaters and anglers. The 26-mile-
long **Lea Valley Regional Park** offers a rich variety of
leisure activities. Also on the Lea is the pretty town of
Ware, the location of the enticing and recently restored
Scott's Grotto, a fantasyland of underground passages
lined with decorative shells, flints and stones, and
created by the Quaker poet John Scott in the 1760s.

7 HENRY MOORE FOUNDATION

Many of the works of England's most renowned
sculptor, who lived from 1898 to 1986, are on display
at the Henry Moore Foundation, which celebrates the
great man's long and productive life. There is also a
collection of Moore's beautiful tapestries in the on-
site Aisled Barn, plus changing exhibits of work from
around the world. Besides attractive gardens, the site
benefits from a tranquil setting amid quintessentially
English countryside. It is open by appointment only.

8 ROYSTON

A favoured hunting base for James I, the charming town of Royston grew up at the intersection of the Icknield Way and Ermine Street, two key Roman highways. Today, its attractions include the award-winning **Priory Gardens** and the intriguing **Royston Cave**. Six miles north and just over the border in Cambridgeshire is **Wimpole Hall**, one of the finest – and largest – stately homes in all East Anglia. Though the house was built in 1640, it was totally revamped in an imposing style in the 18th century. The chapel boasts a renowned *trompe l'oeil* ceiling, while the 15oha (360 acres) of gardens and parkland were landscaped over the years by the combined talents of Charles Bridgeman, Sanderson Miller, Humphry Repton and 'Capability' Brown. **Wimpole Home Farm** was created in 1794 as a then state-of-the-art agricultural estate. Its restored Great Barn now contains a display of farming implements through the ages. There are also a number of rare breed animals.

9 BALDOCK AND HITCHIN

The handsome market town of **Baldock** was founded by the Knights Templar back in the 12th century, and this little gem's charm is largely due to its having escaped rampant redevelopment – most of the buildings in the town centre are at least 100 years old and many date back much further. Neighbouring **Hitchin** has an expansive market square, around which are grouped a substantial number of Tudor, Jacobean and Georgian buildings. Once a staging post set beneath the gentle Pagsdon Hills, Hitchin still has a number of historic and highly atmospheric coaching inns. There is also a large medieval parish church and a late 18th-century priory.

10 SHAW'S CORNER

Tucked away in Ayot St Lawrence, Shaw's Corner is the pretty little Edwardian Arts and Crafts-style villa where Irish-born playwright George Bernard Shaw lived from 1906 until his death in 1950. The modest interior remains just as he left it, with personal effects still in place, while the garden – a haven for wildlife – is an exquisite setting for the revolving summerhouse in which the great man wrote many of his finest works, including *Pygmalion*, on which the popular musical *My Fair Lady* was based.

Take the A505 south west to reach Baldock and, 5 miles further on, Hitchin. 9

Travel south on the B656 and B651, turning left onto unclassified roads after Kimpton to reach Ayot St Lawrence and Shaw's Corner. 10

Follow minor roads south to Wheathampstead, then pick up the B651 south again to return to St Albans.
 1

WITH MORE TIME

Although **Luton and Dunstable**, just over the county border in Bedfordshire, are both quite industrial towns, they are not without their cultural highlights. Luton's Wardown Park Museum celebrates the town's 1,000-year history, while its Stockwood Craft Museum and Gardens bring that past to life with a medieval knot garden, a sculpture garden and a collection of horse-drawn vehicles. Dunstable's 12th-century priory, the place where Henry VIII divorced Catherine of Aragon, is set among the beautiful slopes of Dunstable Downs. Further north, **Wrest Park Gardens** *(left)*, inspired by the great château gardens of the Loire Valley, are well worth a visit.

Arts and learning in Cambridgeshire and Bedfordshire

Rising from the watery flatlands around the Wash to the gentle chalk hills in the south of Bedfordshire, this stretch of countryside is ideal for farming, and much of the land here is given over to agriculture. The result is a green and tranquil landscape dotted with ancient rural towns and villages. In spite of its wealth of cultural interest, the genteel city of Cambridge exudes an equally unhurried air.

TOUR ROUTE

Cambridge ①
Anglesey Abbey ②
Wicken Fen ③
Ely ④
St Ives and Huntingdon ⑤
St Neots ⑥
Bedford ⑦
Old Warden Park ⑧

TOUR LENGTH

DISTANCE approx. 100 miles (160km)

DURATION 3 days

TOURIST INFORMATION CENTRES

BEDFORD St Pauls Square, MK40 1SL; 01234 215226

CAMBRIDGE Wheeler Street, CB2 3QB; 0906 586 2526

ELY Oliver Cromwell's House, 29 St Mary's Street, CB7 4HF; 01353 662062

HUNTINGDON The Library, Princes Street, PE29 3PH; 01480 388588

Clockwise from far left:
Bridge of Sighs, Cambridge;
Wicken Fen Nature Reserve;
Cambridge Botanic Gardens;
carvings, St John's College,
Cambridge; The Backs,
Cambridge

1 CAMBRIDGE

Like its great rival Oxford – known to locals here as 'the other place' – the university city of Cambridge is set beside a delightful river and famous for the beauty of its colleges. The Cam winds through the lawns and gardens known as **The Backs** (as they comprise land at the back of several of the city's colleges), and in summer, punting here is one of life's great languid pleasures.

Cambridge was originally the site of a Roman fort and later a modest Saxon village, but the city you see today was born in 1209, when a riot between 'town and gown' broke out in Oxford. A group of tutors and students fled in fear for their lives and re-convened here, establishing a rival university. Competition between the light and dark blues – Cambridge and Oxford universities, respectively – remains intense to this day.

While the various university colleges *(see p46)* are key sights, the city has a lot more to offer, even though much of it is as a direct result of its role as a centre of learning. The vast **Fitzwilliam Museum**, with its imposing portico supported by 12 columns, is an appropriately grand setting for one of the world's great collections of antiquities from Egypt, Greece and Rome. Also featured are sculpture, furniture, pottery and works of art, with paintings by Titian, Monet, Degas and other great artists. Nearby, a more eclectic collection gathered from around the world occupies the three floors of the **Museum of Archaeology and Anthropology**, including some Pacific artefacts brought back by Captain Scott. The exploits of the great explorer are the focus at the **Scott Polar Research Institute Museum**, accompanied by displays on Arctic and Antarctic exploration and Inuit life. Closer to home, the everyday life of ordinary people from the 17th century to the present day is celebrated at the captivating **Cambridge and County Folk Museum**.

Opened in 1846, the **Cambridge Botanic Garden**, just one of several picturesque gardens in the city, today showcases more than 10,000 plant species within its peaceful 16ha (40 acres). Tours are available year round and need to be booked in advance.

*Head east out of
Cambridge on the A1303
and continue on the B1102
just after crossing the A14.
Turn left onto the
unclassified road to Lode
for **Anglesey Abbey**.*

 2

Clockwise from above:
King's College, Cambridge;
Anglesey Abbey; Wicken Fen;
grounds, Anglesey Abbey;
Trinity College, Cambridge;
King's College Chapel,
Cambridge

CAMBRIDGE'S COLLEGES

The town's 31 colleges were founded by royal, noble and religious patrons, who were wealthy enough to secure the leading architects of the day. This resulted in a legacy of stunning buildings that span some 700 years. Many of the colleges are open to the public part of the year, and some do not charge admission.

The oldest college is **Peterhouse** (1284), which was built by the Bishop of Ely, though only the original hall remains. One of the most famous, and impressive, of all university campuses, **King's College** was founded by King Henry VI in 1441. Its chapel was completed 100 years later and is truly majestic, with a soaring fan-vaulted roof, an ornate oak screen gifted by Henry VIII and Rubens' masterpiece *The Adoration of the Magi*. Visitors are sometimes fortunate enough to catch a rehearsal by the world-famous choir. Henry VIII built **Trinity College** in 1546 and it comprises beautiful Tudor buildings, though the library is a later addition, built by Sir Christopher Wren.

ILLUSTRIOUS ALUMNI

No fewer than 19 British prime ministers, nine Archbishops of Canterbury and 78 Nobel Prize winners were educated – or were tutors – at Cambridge University. The role of honour also includes such notables as Samuel Pepys, Sir Isaac Newton, Lord Byron, A A Milne, Charles Darwin, Stephen Hawking and Prince Charles.

2 ANGLESEY ABBEY

Built in 1600 on the site of an Augustinian priory founded in 1135, Anglesey Abbey is now home to a collection of clocks, paintings and furniture that was amassed by former owner, the 1st Lord Fairhaven, from the 1930s onwards. The gracious 40-ha (98-acre) garden, also created by Lord Fairhaven, is renowned for its herbaceous borders, late winter snowdrops, spring hyacinths and summertime dahlias. An arboretum and a spectacular winter garden, plus an attractive, working 18th-century watermill add to the interest.

3 WICKEN FEN

The flatlands known as the Fens were once a wilderness of marshes, bogs, reedbeds and watercourses that covered much of northern East Anglia. In the 17th and 18th centuries, with the help of Dutch water engineers, most of the area was drained to provide rich, fertile farming lands. Wicken Fen, sometimes called Adventurer's Fen, is one of the few parts that remains in its original wild state. It is easy to picture the legendary Hereward The Wake holding the Normans at bay in the maze of waterways and reed beds here, as he did in the 11th century. Today, this lonely, rather haunting place – Britain's oldest nature reserve – is a favourite haunt of birdwatchers and other nature lovers.

*Return to the B1102 and turn left towards Swaffham Prior. Proceed north on unclassified roads via Reach to **Wicken Fen**.* ③

*Head north to the A1123 and drive west to Stretham, then turn right onto the A10 into **Ely**.*

④

Clockwise from above:
Lantern Tower, Ely Cathedral;
Shuttleworth Collection, Old
Warden Park; stained glass
window, Ely Cathedral

*Take the A142 west to
Sutton and turn left onto
B1381. At the A1123, turn
right and drive via **St Ives***
⑤ *to **Huntingdon**.*

*Head south to
Godmanchester, then take
the unclassified road via*
⑥ *Great Paxton to **St Neots**.*

*Take unclassified roads
west to Bolnhurst, then
head south on the B660
into **Bedford**.*

⑤ ST IVES AND HUNTINGDON

Just down the road is **St Ives**, another riverside gem,
with its splendid 15th-century stone bridge crowned
by one of only a handful of bridge chapels left in the
country. On Market Hill there's a handsome bronze
statue of Oliver Cromwell, who lived in the town
between 1631 and 1636. Markets are still held on
Mondays: those that take place on bank holidays are
especially busy. Nearby, **Houghton Mill** is a wonderfully
well-preserved example of a wooden clapboard water
mill that is still operational. On the B1040, between
St Ives and Somersham, the **Raptor Foundation** is a
sanctuary for owls and other birds of prey that is open
to the public and offers daily flying demonstrations.

Despite having lost its role as an administrative
centre due to the absorbtion of Huntingdonshire into
Cambridgeshire, the former county town of Huntingdon
– the birthplace of Oliver Cromwell – retains an air of
quiet self-importance. Set on the River Great Ouse it
is a handsome place with numerous fine Victorian,
Georgian and older buildings. In the Market Place is
The Thinking Soldier, a statue created by Lady Kathleen
Scott, the widow of Captain Scott.

⑥ ST NEOTS

Cambridgeshire's largest town, St Neots takes its
name from a Cornish saint and was founded in AD974,
growing up around a Saxon priory that once contained
some relics of the saint. These are now held in the finely
decorated 15th-century St Neots Parish Church. The
award-winning **St Neots Museum** relates the town's
long history, while the Riverside Park next to the River
Great Ouse is a haven of tranquillity.

④ ELY

Fanciful observers have likened the towering Ely
Cathedral to a ship sailing across the Fens. This
magnificent edifice is certainly a landmark for miles
around, and the city was at one time completely
surrounded by water. A wonderful example of the
Romanesque style of ecclesiastical architecture,
the present cathedral arose in 1083 on the site of a
monastery founded in AD673 by St Ethelreda. Within
the cathedral is the unique **Stained Glass Museum**.
Around 100 panels show how stained glass has
progressed from the 1200s to modern times. There
are also exhibits showing how stained glass is
designed and made.

Oliver Cromwell, Lord High Protector of England
during the Commonwealth, the period in the 17th
century when England briefly become a republic, lived
in Ely for some time. The half-timbered house to which
he moved in 1636 with mother, sisters, wife and eight
children is now the fascinating **Oliver Cromwell's
House**, which depicts life in his time. Ely's atmospheric
old centre contains numerous old merchants' houses,
and boating on the River Great Ouse is one of the
pleasurable pursuits offered by the city.

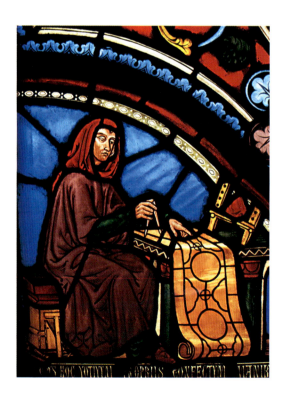

7 BEDFORD

Once a lace-making centre, Bedford is also known for its links with John Bunyan and Glenn Miller: the former was born one mile away at Elstow, while the latter was stationed at a nearby US air base and recorded his radio shows in the town. The town's **John Bunyan Museum** contains displays on the author's life, as well as 169 editions of *The Pilgrim's Progress*, while a museum dedicated to the bandleader can be found at Twinwood Airfield, three miles to the north west.

In the centre of Bedford, the outstanding **Cecil Higgins Art Gallery** was endowed by a rich and benevolent local brewer. A changing collection of water colours, drawings and prints from the Renaissance to modern times includes works by the likes of Gainsborough and Freud, and complements collections of ceramics, glassware and lace all set in a Victorian Mansion and its modern extension. The adjacent former brewery houses the **Bedford Museum**, which traces the area's human history from the Stone Age and features lace-making and farming displays as well as re-created Victorican rooms. **The Embankment**, a promenade running alongside the broad River Great Ouse, is a delightful man-made beauty spot with lovely gardens, water meadows, a Victorian wrought-iron suspension bridge and a bandstand of the same era.

As you head east out of town, you can see the vast hangers built at Cardington to house the ill-fated R101 airship that crashed while on its maiden voyage to India in 1930. Further east, and a little off the tour route, is **Moggerhanger Park**, a Georgian stately home designed by Sir John Soane and set in 13.5ha (33 acres) of parkland.

8 OLD WARDEN PARK

Two miles to the east of Bedford, Old Warden Park is home to the splendid **Shuttleworth Collection**, which celebrates those magnificent men in their flying machines. The 40 aircraft displayed in period hangars located on a former airfield are all in working condition, and range from a 1909 Bleriot to a 1942 Spitfire. The collection also showcases veteran and vintage bicycles, motorcycles and cars plus Victorian horse-drawn carriages. Next door, the lovely **Swiss Garden** was laid out in the early Victorian era and centres around a thatched Swiss Cottage. Adjacent is the **English School of Falconry**, where visitors can see owls, falcons and other birds of prey at the closest of quarters – and even handle them.

Take unclassified roads south east via Cardington. At Old Warden, follow signs to Old Warden Park. **8**

Head east through Biggleswade to pick up the B1040 north, then turn right onto the B1042 and continue on the A603 to return to Cambridge.

 **1**

WITH MORE TIME

Woburn Abbey is one of England's grandest stately homes and residence of the dukes of Bedford since 1547. The house is full of great paintings by the likes of Van Dyck, Gainsborough and Canaletto, as well as rare porcelain and furniture. Its expansive grounds are home to 10 species of deer – and **Woburn Safari Park** *(left)*. Woburn itself is a pretty Georgian village, with period shopfronts and a profusion of antique dealers. Nearby, the narrow-gauge **Leighton Buzzard Railway** provides a delightful steam train experience on tracks laid down in 1919 to serve local industry.

Lincolnshire, Nottinghamshire, Leicestershire, Rutland and Northamptonshire

Wolds, Fens and sweeping skies

With its flat Fens, rolling Wolds and endless fields stretching out under expansive skies, Lincolnshire is essentially an agricultural county. But that doesn't stop 21 million visitors a year from flocking to its historic towns, traditional English seaside resorts and wide open countryside. With the 140-mile Viking Way running across the county, more than 600 miles of waterways cutting through the Wolds and Fens, and an unspoilt coastline of marshes, dunes and golden sands, this is a wonderland for lovers of the great outdoors.

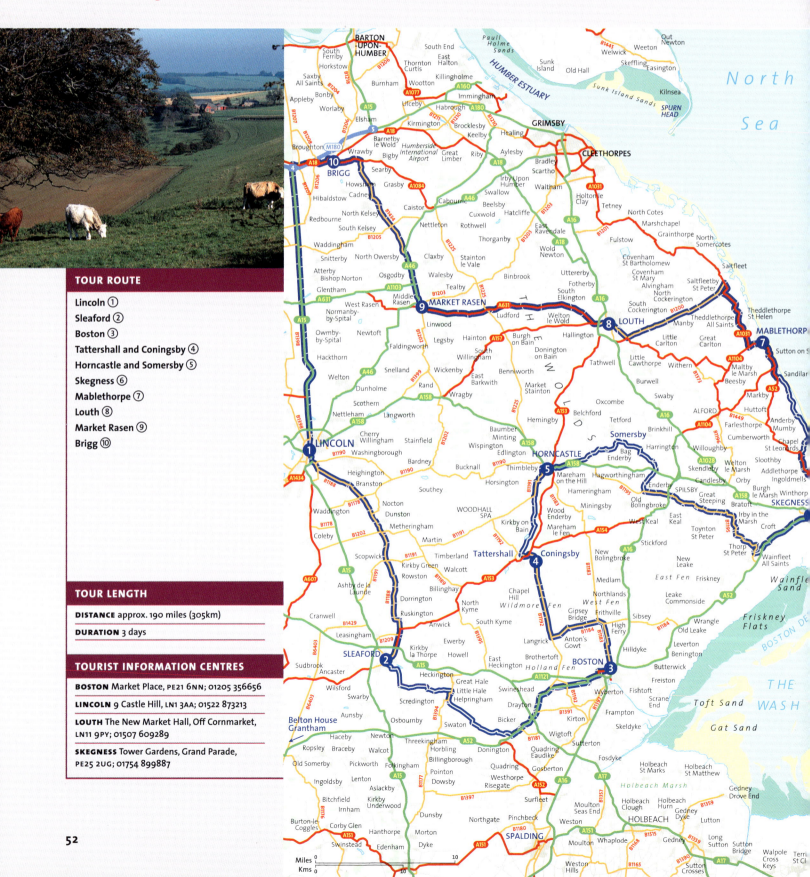

TOUR ROUTE

Lincoln ①
Sleaford ②
Boston ③
Tattershall and Coningsby ④
Horncastle and Somersby ⑤
Skegness ⑥
Mablethorpe ⑦
Louth ⑧
Market Rasen ⑨
Brigg ⑩

TOUR LENGTH

DISTANCE approx. 190 miles (305km)

DURATION 3 days

TOURIST INFORMATION CENTRES

BOSTON Market Place, PE21 6NN; 01205 356656

LINCOLN 9 Castle Hill, LN1 3AA; 01522 873213

LOUTH The New Market Hall, Off Cornmarket, LN11 9PY; 01507 609289

SKEGNESS Tower Gardens, Grand Parade, PE25 2UG; 01754 899887

Clockwise from far left:
**view of the Wolds; view of the
Lincolnshire Fen; Lincoln city
centre; gardens at Springfield,
Spalding; Lincoln Cathedral**

1 LINCOLN

Lincoln's magnificent **cathedral**, commissioned by William the Conqueror in 1072, dominates the horizon for miles around. Its 82m-tall central tower (270ft), though only half its original height since its spire was toppled in a storm in 1549, is still one of the highest in England. Inside the cathedral, look out for the mischievous Lincoln Imp, a stone carving perched at the top of a pillar near the angel choir. Close by, the city's Norman **castle** now contains one of only four surviving copies of King John's Magna Carta. Many of the displays here relate to the building's later use as a prison – such as the pews in the chapel, which were designed to keep prisoners in solitary confinement. Just to the south of the cathedral is the atmospheric ruin of the **Medieval Bishop's Palace**. Though gutted by Parliamentary forces during the Civil War, this grand old building is still an imposing reminder of the church's importance in medieval Britain. Its grounds contain one of Europe's most northerly vineyards. At the bottom of the appropriately named Steep Hill – a narrow, cobbled street lined with attractive medieval buildings – is the 900-year-old Jew's House, now a restaurant.

Opened in 2005, The Collection is a state-of-the-art museum and exhibition space focusing on archaeology and art from the Stone Age right through to the present day. It is linked to the ever-popular **Usher Gallery**. The more established **Museum of Lincolnshire Life** takes an evocative look at the city's more recent social history. Features include a working Victorian printing press and a collection of agricultural implements.

*Leave Lincoln on the B1188
south for 14 miles to join
the A153 into Sleaford.*

3 BOSTON

Always a great trading centre, Boston was a lively port in the 13th century and is a bustling market town today. It has a compact medieval centre, with two main streets following the north and south banks of the river, and smaller lanes and alleys running in between. Popularly known as Boston Stump, the massive 82m-tall tower (270ft) of the 14th-century **St Botolph's Church**, built in 1309, is one of eastern England's most famous landmarks, and is visible for many miles around. The effort of climbing the tower's 365 steps brings the reward of views reaching as far as Lincoln, 30 miles away.

A little outside the town, the **Pilgrim Fathers Memorial** marks the spot from where, in 1607, a group of puritan Protestants attempted to flee in search of religious freedom in the Netherlands. Their two ringleaders were tried at the 15th-century **Boston Guildhall**, where the courtroom and cells in which they were held can still be visited today. The group eventually made it via Harwich, London and Plymouth to Massachusetts – where they established a village called Plymouth and, later, the city that now shares Boston's name.

Much later, in 1819, the **Maud Foster Windmill** was built. The tallest working mill in the country, it is arranged over seven storeys and, rather unusually, has five sails. It's worth a climb to the top for some wonderful views over the surrounding fenland scenery. Boston's other architectural talking points include the **Blackfriars** (a former Dominican friary), the 18th-century merchant's home **Fydell House**, and **Hussey Tower**. The last is an early brick tower – once part of a larger house – built in the mid-15th century and home to nobleman Lord John Hussey until he was executed for treason following the Lincolnshire Rebellion in 1536.

Follow unclassified roads south east to pick up the A52 at Drayton. From there it is a 5-mile drive north east into Boston.

2 SLEAFORD

The Hub, a former riverside grain warehouse, has recently been converted into the largest gallery space for contemporary arts outside London. But in spite of this injection of cutting-edge design, the ancient market town of Sleaford still oozes history. The pretty 12th-century parish church of St Denys looks out over the market place, where markets now take place three times weekly, on Mondays, Fridays and Saturdays. Also in the town centre is the Black Bull pub, which has an old wall-sign depicting bull-baiting – a sport that was last seen here in the early 19th century.

Set in a pleasant location on the banks of the River Slea, the fully operational **Cogglesford Watermill** offers visitors the opportunity to watch milling demonstrations and buy organic stone-ground flour produced on site, while Grade II-listed **Navigation House** is a one-time canal office where the history of trade on the river is explained through interactive displays. Four miles north west of the town, the **Cranwell Aviation Heritage Centre** tells the story of Cranwell College, the world's first military air academy, which opened its doors in 1920.

Drive north on the B1183 and then west on the B1184 to Langrick. From here it is an 8-mile journey north on the B1192 to Coningsby.

4 TATTERSHALL AND CONINGSBY

A fortified manor house with a 30m-high square keep (100ft), **Tattershall Castle** is one of the finest examples of medieval brickwork in the country. Together with the imposing **Holy Trinity Church**, which stands alongside, it was commissioned by Ralph Cromwell, the Treasurer of England, in the 15th century. The church is a magnificent example of the Perpendicular style, and boasts some of the finest medieval stained glass in England.

Neighbouring **Coningsby** has another notable building: **St Michael's Church** has the largest surviving one-handed clock, which dates from the 17th century. However, Coningsby is best known today for its RAF base and the aerial display group known as the **Battle of Britain Memorial Flight**. Usually consisting of an Avro Lancaster, a Supermarine Spitfire and a Hawker Hurricane, the flight is well known for participating in air shows and fly-pasts all over the country. Its base has a visitor centre offering tours of the hangars – and guests who time their visit well are treated to spectacular views of the aircraft setting off for events.

Take the minor road north through Kirkby on Bain to the B1191, which leads you north east into *Horncastle*. *Somersby*, to the north east of the town, can be reached on minor roads. **5**

5 HORNCASTLE AND SOMERSBY

The Romans established a fort in **Horncastle** towards the end of their occupation. Since then, this has been a pleasant but sleepy backwater – it is renowned today for its antiques shops. Four miles to the east is the site of the Civil War Battle of Winceby, fought in 1643. To the east is the village of **Somersby**, birthplace of Alfred, Lord Tennyson. Although the interior of the poet's beautiful childhood home is rarely opened to the public, many visitors stop by to explore the village and discover his 'haunts of ancient peace'.

Drive south on minor roads to meet the B1195 eastbound to Wainfleet All Saints. Here you can join the A52 north east to reach *Skegness*.

6

Clockwise from far left:
St Botolph's Church, Boston;
sundial, Somersby church;
Tattershall Castle; Maud
Foster Windmill, Boston

Follow the A52 north again, detouring via Chapel St Leonards onto the unclassified coast road. This rejoins the A52 at Sandilands for the short stretch into **Mablethorpe**.

7

6 SKEGNESS

Known affectionately by its fans as 'Skeggy', the popular east coast resort of Skegness was founded as a timber port during the Viking era, but remained a small place with a population of well under 1,000 until the arrival of the railway in 1873. After that, however, it began to attract hordes of working-class day-trippers – giving the Earl of Scarborough the idea of creating a purpose-built seaside resort. Construction began on tree-lined avenues, gardens, a park and a pier at the end of the 19th century. By the 1920s the town had become a major holiday destination for industrial workers, prompting the local council to add an array of amenities, including a boating lake, an amusement park, bowling greens, rose gardens and a bathing pool – all of which survive today, albeit in a state of somewhat faded glory. In addition, the town now has an entertainment centre and a varied collection of tourist attractions including the **Church Farm Museum** of rural life, the **Natureland Seal Sanctuary**, the **National Parrot Sanctuary** and some magnificent walled gardens at **Gunby Hall**. Three miles south of the town, the peninsula of **Gibraltar Point** is a popular 530-ha (1,300-acre) nature reserve overlooking the Wash. Its sand dunes and salt marshes are a haven for migratory birds.

7 MABLETHORPE

Mablethorpe and neighbouring **Sutton on Sea** are unprepossessing traditional seaside resorts, but this part of the Lincolnshire coast offers more than just a bucket-and-spade experience. In addition to the many fine walks along the beaches and foreshore there is the **Saltfleetby and Theddlethorpe Dunes Reserve**, which runs five miles north from here: a wilderness of sand dunes and fresh- and saltwater marshes crisscrossed by hiking paths.

Take the A1031 north for 4 miles, then turn left to join the B1200 into **Louth**.

8

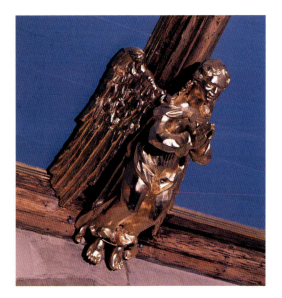

Follow signs for the A631, which is a straight 15-mile run to **Market Rasen**.

 **9**

SKEGNESS IS SO BRACING

The familiar 'So bracing' slogan, thought up by an unknown member of railway staff, was combined with the famous cartoon-like image of the Jolly Fisherman, drawn by John Hassall in 1908, to give Skegness a hugely successful advertising campaign. Commissioned by the Great Northern Railway Company, Hassall was paid just 12 guineas for his marketing masterpiece.

8 LOUTH

The Greenwich Meridian passes through the middle of Louth, placing this pleasant Georgian market town both in the western hemisphere and in the eastern. The exact location of the meridian line is marked with a small plaque on Eastgate, and its presence here also provided the inspiration for three sculptures on the **Louth Art Trail**. The town takes its name from the River Lud and once had some 13 watermills, the story of which is told at the excellent **Louth Museum**. Other unique exhibits on display at the same venue include works by the local 19th-century wood carver Thomas Wilkinson Wallis and the architectural designs of James Fowler – both of whom are also commemorated by blue plaques in the town.

Once a centre of the wool trade, Louth is renowned for its expansive open market place, which hosted massive eight-day fairs during the Middle Ages and still attracts dozens of stalls on market days (Wednesdays, Fridays and Saturdays). Its most dominant architectural feature is the soaring spire of the 16th-century **St James' Church**, and from here it's just a short stroll along Westgate, an elegant thoroughfare lined with Georgian townhouses, to **Westgate Fields** – a pretty open space and another top location on the town's art trail. Louth's location at the foot of the rolling Lincolnshire Wolds makes it a superb base for walking, mountain biking and horse riding in the surrounding countryside.

Clockwise from above:
**countryside between
Horncastle and Skegness;
Market Rasen sign; plaster
angel decoration in St
James' Church, Louth**

9 MARKET RASEN

A traditional small market town, with buildings mainly of Georgian and Victorian provenance, Market Rasen is noted for its attractive period shop fronts and the 19th-century **Centenary Chapel**, with its stone columns and brick façade. However, this part of the world is better known for **Market Rasen Racecourse**, host to a busy programme of National Hunt events that attract steeplechasing fans from across the country.

10 BRIGG

Taking its name from the bridge over the River Ancholme, Brigg has long been a busy market centre. A Royal Charter for its annual horse fair was first granted by King John some 800 years ago, and it is an event that still survives today, taking place in early August. There is also a weekly (Thursday) market selling high-quality local produce. The little streets called The Courts take their names from the artisans who used to work there – the principle one being Coney Court, where rabbit skins (one of Brigg's most lucrative exports during the 18th century) were cured. While the units have now been given over to shops, the emphasis remains firmly on specialist local outlets rather than the all-too-familiar high street chains. The carved angel on the **Angel Hotel**'s balcony is said to be 125 years old, but the building was important as far back as the days when Oliver Cromwell and his army roamed these lands.

*Follow the A46 north,
forking left onto the B1434
and then turning left onto
the A1084 to reach the
centre of Brigg.* **10**

ERMINE STREET

One of the four main roads of Saxon England, Ermine Street (now the A15) was originally built by the Romans to connect London with the important garrison towns of Lincoln and York. It is sometimes known as The Old North Road, distinguishing it from the A1 Great North Road, which runs nearly parallel. It is an interesting – and very direct – way to return to Lincoln.

*Take the A18 west towards
Scunthorpe, then, at the
motorway junction, join the
A15. This takes you south in
a dead straight line for some
23 miles, with just one kink,
to return to Lincoln.*
1

WITH MORE TIME

To the south of the tour, the flower-growing capital of England, **Spalding** *(left)*, is an attractive town set by the River Welland. It is ringed by bulb-growing fields and renowned for its acres of daffodils and tulips each spring. May's Flower Festival is a riot of colour, and the beautiful show gardens at Springfields include creations by the likes of Charlie Dimmock and Kim Wilde. Just north of Grantham, **Belton House** also has stunning gardens, plus collections of tapestries, portraits and fine furniture. **Grantham** itself is perhaps best known as the birthplace of Margaret Thatcher.

Nottinghamshire: the heart of merrie England

Most of Nottinghamshire once fell within the boundaries of the vast Sherwood Forest, and there are still great swathes of unspoilt countryside remaining to this day. Redolent with legends of Robin Hood and his fellow outlaws, this is a place strongly associated with folklore and legend – but the many historic castles and battlefields provide ample opportunity for visitors to discover the real and turbulent history of the area.

TOUR ROUTE

- Newark on Trent ①
- Belvoir Castle ②
- Ruddington ③
- Thrumpton ④
- Wollaton Hall and Park ⑤
- Eastwood ⑥
- Newstead Abbey ⑦
- Hardwick Hall ⑧
- Sherwood Forest Country Park ⑨
- Clumber Park ⑩
- Worksop ⑪
- West Markham ⑫
- Cromwell ⑬

TOUR LENGTH

DISTANCE approx. 140 miles (225km)

DURATION 3 days

TOURIST INFORMATION CENTRES

NEWARK The Gilstrap Centre, Castlegate, NG24 1BG; 01636 655765

NOTTINGHAM 1–4 Smithy Row, NG1 2BY; 0115 915 5330

WORKSOP Worksop Library, Memorial Avenue, S80 2BP; 01909 501148

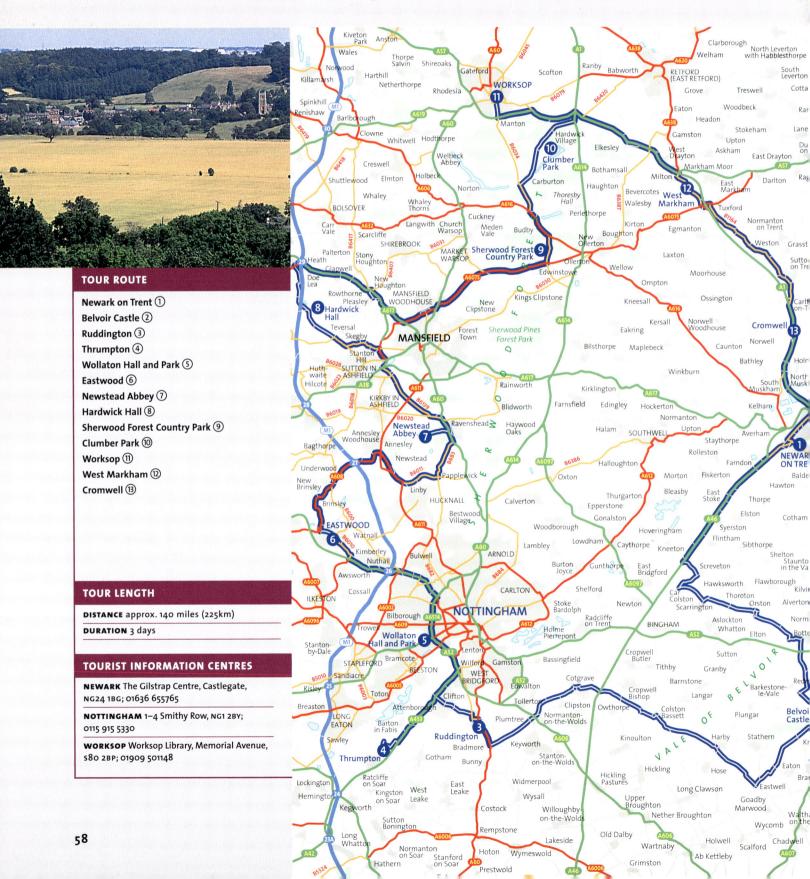

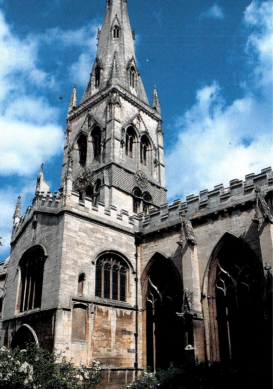

Clockwise from far left:
Vale of Belvoir; Vale of
Belvoir; the River Trent and
Newark Castle; church of St
Mary Magdalene, Newark

1 NEWARK ON TRENT

Picturesque 14th-century half-timbered buildings – among them the former hotel where soon-to-be prime minister William Ewart Gladstone made his first political speech – line the large cobbled market square in the centre of Newark. Just a stone's throw away, romantically set in landscaped gardens on the bank of the River Trent, stands the ruin of the once formidable **Newark Castle**. This is where King John died in 1216, a little more than a year after signing the Magna Carta. More famously, it was a royalist stronghold and the scene of a long siege during the final stages of the Civil War. Only around a fifth of this imposing building remains, the rest having been destroyed by Oliver Cromwell in 1646 following the castle's final surrender. However, the impressive three-storey Romanesque gatehouse and the massive earthworks raised during those troubled Civil War days remain largely intact.

The majestic parish church of St Mary Magdalene is one of the finest in the country, and also one of the tallest – its spire dominates the landscape for miles around. The town also has some worthwhile museums, including the **Millgate Museum**, housed in an old mill, which focuses on the life of the town and its people – from working conditions to domestic life – during the 19th and 20th centuries. Its War Gallery spans the period from 1914–1945 and features an evocative re-creation of a 1940s family living room. To the north of the town, at Winthorpe airfield, is **Newark Air Museum**, home to one of Europe's finest displays of British, European and American aircraft, while **Newark Showground** offers a year-round programme of events ranging from vast antiques fairs to a popular real ale festival.

*Leave Newark on Trent and take the historic A46 Fosse Way south west for 10 miles. Turn left for Screveton and follow the lanes via Car Colston, Orston and Bottesford to **Belvoir Castle**.*

 ⟶ • • • • • • • • • • • ❷

Clockwise from above:
Belvoir Castle; portrait
of Lord Byron, Newstead
Abbey; Wollaton Hall

Drive west through the Vale
of Belvoir on unclassified
lanes, taking in Eastwell,
Cotgrave and Bradmore,
3 to reach **Ruddington**.

Drive west on minor roads,
then take the A453 south
for 4 miles to reach
4 **Thrumpton**.

Backtrack up the A453
to join the Nottingham
bypass, heading north
west for 3 miles to get
5 to **Wollaton Hall**.

Rejoin the bypass, heading
north to the junction with
the A610. Cross the M1 on
this road, forking right at
Kimberley onto the B6010
to reach **Eastwood**.

2 BELVOIR CASTLE

Half a mile over the county border in Leicestershire, the present Belvoir Castle (pronounced 'beaver'), completed in the early 19th century, is the fourth to be built on the site, the previous three having been destroyed during the Wars of the Roses, the English Civil War and a major fire in 1816. Home to the dukes and duchesses of Rutland for some 1,000 years and still inhabited by them today, the castle's notable interior features tapestries, porcelain, silks and sculptures as well as pictures by Holbein, Reynolds, Gainsborough and Poussin. The castle also contains the regimental museum of the Queen's Royal Lancers. Outside are gently sloping lawns and a collection of statues set into the hillside, plus the Duchess's Spring Gardens, a magical woodland hideaway with a natural spring that was created at the beginning of the 19th century.

VALE OF BELVOIR

This is the heart of the Shires, a rural patchwork of fields, woods and picturesque stone villages. The name means 'beautiful view' and that's an appropriate tag. Settlements like Eastwell, Orston and Harby have enormous charm, while hikers and bikers can get away from it all and follow the delightful towpath of the Grantham Canal.

3 RUDDINGTON

Ruddington's **Nottingham Transport Heritage Centre** occupies more than 4.5ha (11 acres) within a delightful country park. There's a railway and bus museum, plus a stretch of restored rail track offering rides to visitors. Two miles from Ruddington is **Attenborough**, which has a well-proportioned church and neatly manicured graveyard. Henry Ireton, one of Oliver Cromwell's most famous generals, was baptised here in 1611.

4 THRUMPTON

The Powdrill family, owners of the original 12th-century house at Thrumpton, forfeited their home and property as a result of their implication in the Gunpowder Plot. The present **Thrumpton Hall**, built in the 17th century, is most notable for its exquisite woodwork – similar to the work of the great Grinling Gibbons, though the craftsman here is unknown. The three-storey ornamental staircase, made from wood felled on the estate, is a particular highlight. Note that tours of the house are by appointment only. Close by are **Ratcliffe on Soar**, today dominated by its vast coal-fired power station (where you can take a guided tour), and **Kingston on Soar**, with its little church. Inside the church is another piece of elaborate carving, this time in the shape of a canopy supported on four decorative pillars. The piece stands alone now, but is said to have once belonged to the tomb of one of the historic local families.

5 WOLLATON HALL AND PARK

Wollaton Hall is an imposing Tudor mansion set in 200ha (500 acres) of mature parkland, where herds of red and fallow deer roam. It was built in 1588 by coal magnate Sir Francis Willoughby. Attractions include a natural history museum; an industrial museum with exhibits including lace-making equipment, Raleigh bicycles and a huge 1858 beam engine; and the yard gallery with displays themed around the interface of art and the environment. There is also a lovely ornamental lake. Although the estate is under refurbishment until 2007, some attractions will be open to visitors throughout.

6 EASTWOOD

The world of controversial novelist, poet and artist D H Lawrence is brought to life at the **D H Lawrence Birthplace Museum**, set in the house where he was born on 11 September 1885: a cramped miner's cottage typical of the area. The **craft centre** next door showcases the remarkable wooden sculptures of local artist Elaine Thompson. Outside, the **Blue Line Trail**, marked with a blue line along the pavement, guides you to the other houses Lawrence lived in, as well as to eight other sites relating to his life and times. As a boy, the writer of *Lady Chatterley's Lover* used to pick up his father's wages from the offices of local coal mine owners Barber, Walker and Co. Now renovated, these premises operate as the **Durban House Heritage Centre**, which has exhibits relating to the town and its mining community during the Victorian era, along with changing exhibits of contemporary art.

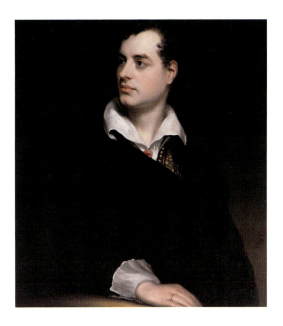

*Take the A608 northbound, turning right onto the A611, then forking left onto the B6011. At Papplewick, turn left onto the B683 and left again onto the A60. The turning for **Newstead Abbey** is on the left after 1 mile.* **7**

7 NEWSTEAD ABBEY

Originally a monastic house founded in the late 12th-century, Newstead Abbey became the seat of the Byron family in 1540. By 1818, the building had fallen into disrepair and the poet Lord Byron was forced to sell it to his good friend Colonel Thomas Wildman. Newstead was restored to its former glory, but remained a private home until 1931, when it was gifted to Nottingham Corporation for the enjoyment of the public. Set amid 120 glorious hectares (300 acres) of parkland and gardens, with ponds, water features and a tranquil Japanese garden, the house is richly furnished and now contains Byron memorabilia.

8 HARDWICK HALL

One of the most spectacular and complete Elizabethan houses in England, Hardwick Hall was built at the behest of the powerful and immensely rich Bess of Hardwick, a lady as formidable as Queen Elizabeth I herself. This truly stately pile is jam-packed with treasures, including a significant collection of 16th- and 17th-century tapestries and embroideries. In addition to expansive parklands, there are orchards and herb gardens to explore, and rare-breed cattle and sheep to admire.

*Continue north on the A60, then west on the B6020 and north on the B6139, joining the B6014 at Sutton in Ashfield. Proceed to Stanton Hill, then take minor roads to reach **Hardwick Hall**.* **8**

*Head north to Heath and turn onto the A617 towards Mansfield. Turn onto the A6075 east and continue to Edwinstowe, turning onto the B6034 for the **Sherwood Forest Country Park** visitor centre.* **9**

9 SHERWOOD FOREST COUNTRY PARK

Once the haunt of the legendary Robin Hood and his merry men, the Sherwood Forest of today is much reduced from the royal hunting grounds that once covered many thousands of hectares. Encompassing 180ha (450 acres) of the surviving oak and silver birch woodlands, Sherwood Forest Country Park's **Visitor Centre**, situated next to the massive and venerable Major Oak, offers exhibitions and waymarked forest trails. There is also a programme of events that includes a Robin Hood Festival each summer. Two miles west is the **Sherwood Forest Farm Park**, which is home to 40 different varieties of threatened farm animals – from kune pigs and water buffalo to ornamental ducks and wildfowl. Lose yourself in the pleasant and peaceful surroundings – the beautiful water gardens are an attraction in themselves.

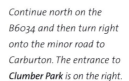

*Continue north on the B6034 and then turn right onto the minor road to Carburton. The entrance to **Clumber Park** is on the right.*

THE DUKERIES

A small district within Sherwood Forest, the Dukeries earned its name because it once contained the homes of five dukes: the dukes of Portland, Newcastle, Kingston, Norfolk and Leeds. Today, the Duke of Portland, at Welbeck, and Earl Manvers (descendant of the dukes of Kingston), at Thoresby, are still in residence.

Clockwise from below: the Major Oak, Sherwood Forest Country Park; interior of Mr Straw's House, Worksop

10 CLUMBER PARK

Built in 1772 and once among Britain's greatest stately homes, Clumber Park suffered a catastrophic fire in 1879 and what remained of the house was demolished in 1938. All that stands on the estate now is a magnificent stable block, which houses a formidable art collection as well as a pleasant tearoom, a shop and a superb Gothic-inspired chapel resembling a scaled-down cathedral. Laid out by the formidable 'Capability' Brown, the 1,538ha (3,800 acres) of idyllic parkland can be explored on foot or by bicycle. There is also a beautiful lake and superb walled gardens.

11 WORKSOP

Worksop is a no-nonsense Midlands working town, which makes it the perfect setting for its best attraction, **Mr Straw's House** – a pickled-in-aspic 1920s tradesman's home. Incredibly, the property was kept unchanged by the two sons of grocer William Straw and his wife Florence until 1990, when it was handed over to the National Trust. Besides its original Victorian furnishings and Edwardian wallpaper, there are displays of family costume, letters and photos, and a suburban garden typical of the period.

12 WEST MARKHAM

Though just half a mile off the bustling A1 trunk road, West Markham is a peaceful spot that somehow gives the impression of being deep in the country. Its most obvious attraction is perhaps the pretty little 11th-century **All Saints church**. Sadly this fell into disrepair in 1843, and the role of parish church was adopted by a monumental mausoleum built by the Duke of Newcastle to house his family relics. The treasures of this 'new church' include the family vault, a monument to the fourth Duke and a statue dedicated to the memory of his Duchess – who bore him 14 children. This building became redundant as a place of worship in 1971, however, when, rather ironically, the title of parish church passed back to the now-refurbished All Saints.

13 CROMWELL

The village of Cromwell is best known for its charming **Vina Cooke Museum of Dolls and Bygone Childhood**, which has a huge collection of Victorian dolls, prams, cots and toys, plus handmade character dolls depicting film stars and members of the royal family. The collection is housed in a delightful 17th-century dower house, which is itself of considerable interest, being a classic of its era.

Take minor roads north from Clumber and turn left onto the A614, then left again onto the A57. At Manton, turn right for Worksop town centre. **11**

Take the A57 east for 6 miles, then follow the A1 south for the same distance before turning right onto the B1164 to West Markham. **12**

Continue south on the B1164 to Carlton-on-Trent, returning to the A1 for the final mile into Cromwell. **13**

Drive south again on the A1 and follow signs back into Newark on Trent.

 **1**

WITH MORE TIME

Nottingham is a fast-living, trendy place with a sharp eye for fashion: Paul Smith is a native son. The city's castle, a 17th-century mansion built on the site of a Norman fortress, has magnificent interiors and commands great views over the city. Nearby is a network of underground caves *(left)*, through which visitors can take guided tours. Other attractions include the outstanding Galleries of Justice museum, the historic Lace Market area – now packed with modern bars, restaurants and boutiques – and the grandiose city hall, which dominates Nottingham's main square.

Canals, lakes and country estates in Leicestershire and Rutland

Tradition reigns in Leicestershire and Rutland, a real countryside haven where hunting, shooting, fishing and other time-honoured ways of life persist. The soft, undulating hills and fields are crisscrossed with tiny rivers and canals and dotted with lakes and reservoirs that attract abundant wildlife, while a scattering of impressive stately homes sit comfortably alongside bustling market towns and picturesque villages.

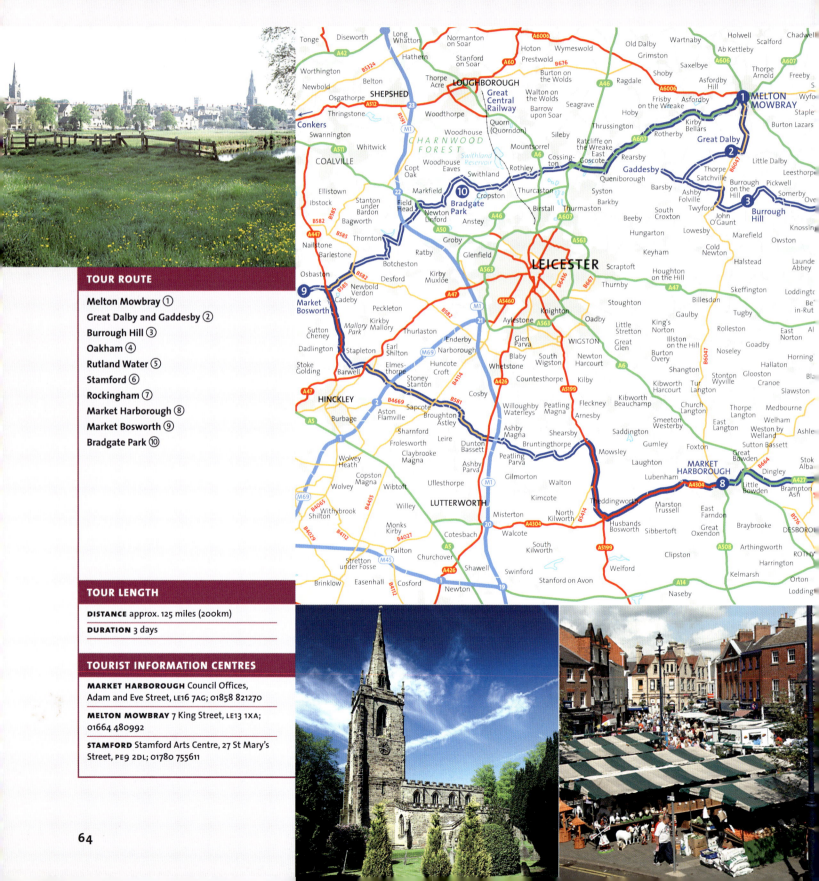

TOUR ROUTE

Melton Mowbray ①

Great Dalby and Gaddesby ②

Burrough Hill ③

Oakham ④

Rutland Water ⑤

Stamford ⑥

Rockingham ⑦

Market Harborough ⑧

Market Bosworth ⑨

Bradgate Park ⑩

TOUR LENGTH

DISTANCE approx. 125 miles (200km)

DURATION 3 days

TOURIST INFORMATION CENTRES

MARKET HARBOROUGH Council Offices, Adam and Eve Street, LE16 7AG; 01858 821270

MELTON MOWBRAY 7 King Street, LE13 1XA; 01664 480992

STAMFORD Stamford Arts Centre, 27 St Mary's Street, PE9 2DL; 01780 755611

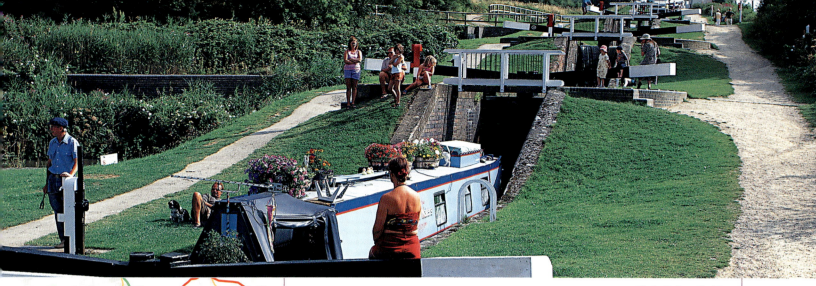

1 MELTON MOWBRAY

Stilton cheese and pork pies are the calling cards of this ancient Leicestershire market town. The cheese is actually named after a village some 25 miles away, but that's because it was once marketed from a coaching inn there – it has always been made in Melton. The **Melton Carnegie Museum** has interesting displays on cheese- and pork-pie-making, plus a wealth of other local history exhibits and a rather controversial section covering the history of fox hunting in the area. One of the town's oldest buildings is **Anne of Cleves' House**, so named because it was gifted by Henry VIII to his fourth wife on their divorce, which has now been converted to a pub. Just 10 minutes' walk from the town centre is the 55-ha (140-acre) **Melton Country Park**, which boasts a lake, a disused railway line that's now a pleasant footpath, and the 40 commemorative oaks that line Queen Elizabeth II's Anniversary Avenue.

Melton Mowbray has been known for its markets for more than 1,000 years, and they still form an important part of the town's culture today. Historically, different types of produce were sold at different locations in the town, each of which was originally marked with a 'cross'. The main spot, in the central Market Place, was reserved for the butter market: this is where dairy products – including the famous Stilton cheese – and eggs were sold right up to the beginning of the 20th century. The original crosses are long gone, but the Butter Cross and Corn Cross have recently been reconstructed on their original sites, while the Sage Cross survives in a street name. These days, you will still find markets trading almost every day of the week, and while most of them are now held in a covered market hall, the Tuesday and Saturday street markets still attract impressive crowds to the town centre, as do the bric-a-brac stalls on Wednesdays.

Clockwise from far left:
view towards Stamford;
Foxton Locks; Anne of Cleves'
House, Melton Mowbray;
view of street market,
Melton Mowbray; church,
Market Bosworth

From Melton Mowbray,
take the B6047 south to
Great Dalby and then turn
right along unclassified
roads to reach Gaddesby.

Clockwise from above:
Burghley House; interior,
Burghley House; Normanton
Church, Rutland Water

2 GREAT DALBY AND GADDESBY

A few miles from Melton Mowbray, **Great Dalby** has
a pleasant village green and a 14th-century church
whose tower is topped by a distinctive pointed roof.
Of more interest, however, is neighbouring **Gaddesby**,
which dates from a Danish settlement of the ninth
century. The Norman **St Luke's Church** has some ornate
carvings in stone and wood – including 15th-century
oak pews and a limestone font. There is also a peal
of eight bells, the oldest of which is dated 1562, and
a dramatic statue of Colonel Cheney, a one-time
resident of nearby Gaddesby Hall who had no fewer
than four horses shot from under him at the Battle
of Waterloo. On the corner of Chapel Lane and Cross
Street stands the Blue Stone, which is said to mark
the spot where John Wesley once preached.

*Return to the B6047 at
Thorpe Satchville, travel
south for 1 mile and then
east again through the
lanes to Burrough Hill.* ③

3 BURROUGH HILL

Enclosing some 8ha (20 acres), the hill fort on Burrough
Hill dates from the early Bronze Age and is strategically
placed atop a Jurassic ridge, with sweeping views in every
direction. It is one of a series of Bronze and Iron Age hill
forts in the area, with other notable examples including
Sconsborough Hill, Ranksborough Hill and Whatborough
Hill. Archaeological digs at Burrough Hill have yielded a
number of important finds, including pottery and three
skeletons – one of them holding a short sword. Fairs and
sports events were held on the hill in Victorian times.
These days, it is popular with walkers and kite-flyers.

*Travel east to Langham,
where you can pick up
the A606 for the last
few miles into Oakham.*

→ • • • • • • • • • • ④

SO MUCH IN SO LITTLE

Having been amalgamated into Leicestershire
in 1974, tiny Rutland – far and away England's
smallest county – regained its independence in
the 1997 local government reforms, largely as a
result of concerted pressure from the public.
Much of the county is covered by Rutland Water,
which vies with Kielder Water in Northumberland
for the title of Europe's largest man-made lake.
Multum in parvo ('So much in so little') is
Rutland's highly apposite motto.

4 OAKHAM

Compact Oakham, the county town of equally compact Rutland, is also, rather fittingly, the birthplace of one the smallest men ever to live in England. Jeffery Hudson, born in 1619, grew only to around 105cm (3ft 6in) tall, and is commemorated with a Blue Plaque on the cottage where he lived. All that remains of **Oakham Castle**, built by a Norman nobleman around 1190, is its mighty Great Hall. More than 200 horseshoes hang on the walls here, the custom being that any visiting peer of the realm must, on his first visit, forfeit a horseshoe to the lord of the manor. The oldest dates from 1470, and the most recent was presented by Prince Charles in 2003.

As the administrative centre of Rutland, this delightful town is also home to the **Rutland County Museum**, housed in an attractive ironstone building. Its collection covers every aspect of local life and history, but it is mainly concerned with the traditional trades of the region: there is a large exhibit of agricultural tools, plus displays on occupations such as coopery, farriery, shoemaking and brewing. Three miles to the west, **Barnsdale Gardens** was the home patch of Geoff Hamilton, presenter of BBC2's Gardener's World, until his death in 1996; the impressive series of 37 different gardens that he designed for the programme is now open to the public.

5 RUTLAND WATER

The 1,254ha (3,100 acres) of Rutland Water are a mecca for watersports and wildlife enthusiasts, the latter drawn by the winter presence of more than 20,000 migratory wildfowl. When the reservoir was created in the 1970s, the attractive sandstone **Normanton Church**, built in 1826, was deemed worth saving. Today it stands below water level, and is saved from flooding only by a specially constructed dyke. Reached via a causeway, the church now houses an interesting local life museum.

6 STAMFORD

Straddling the pretty River Welland, Stamford is one of England's most picturesque towns, full of golden sandstone buildings and cobbled streets. Fine Tudor, Jacobean and Georgian houses are all to be found here, along with some notable crafts and collectibles shops. The history of the town and of the local Stamford Ware pottery is documented by the **Stamford Museum**, which also displays a fully-clothed model of Daniel Lambert *(see box)*. South of Stamford is the ornate Tudor pile of **Burghley House** – venue of the famous horse trials. Built by Queen Elizabeth I's trusted advisor William Cecil between 1565 and 1587, it is one of England's largest and most extravagant stately homes. The combination of gilded staterooms and collections of paintings by Verrio, Gainsborough and Brueghels with the vast kitchens gives a real flavour of upstairs/downstairs life in the country.

DANIEL LAMBERT

This former Leicester jailkeeper died in Stamford in 1809, aged 39, and is buried in the local St Martin's churchyard. By the time of his death, he weighed a phenomenal 333kg (52st 11lbs) – and was so large that a wall of the house in which he died had to be dismantled so that the 20 pallbearers could lift his coffin out. Towards the end of his lifetime, Lambert had chosen to profit from his extraordinary size by exhibiting himself as a curiosity, and his name soon came to be identified with vast size – the writer George Meredith, for example, famously described London as 'the Daniel Lambert of cities'.

Leave Oakham on the A606 east, which takes you along the north shore of Rutland Water, and past several parking spots. For Normanton Church, turn right onto minor roads after Empingham.  **5**

Continue west on the A606 all the way into Stamford. **6**

Take the A6121 south west, crossing the A47 to join the B672 after 9 miles. At Caldecott turn left onto the A6003 to reach Rockingham.
 **7**

Clockwise from above:
Rockingham Castle; plaque,
Bosworth Battlefield; battle
reconstruction, Bosworth
Battlefield; River Lin, Bradgate
Park; trees, Rockingham
Castle; Foxton Locks

7 ROCKINGHAM

William the Conqueror commissioned **Rockingham Castle**
to dominate the strategically important Welland Valley,
and it remained an important royal seat throughout
the Middle Ages – when kings used to come here for
the hunting in Rockingham Forest. King John spent
much of his time at the castle, and his treasure chest
still stands in the Great Hall, giving rise to the suspicion
that his lost crown jewels may lie buried here rather
than in the Wash, as is traditionally believed. Although
it has been used as a family home since Tudor times,
Rockingham is one of the country's best-preserved
medieval castles both outside and in, and many of its
paintings and furnishings are original. Surrounding the
ramparts, with their views across five counties, are 5ha
(12 acres) of sweeping lawns and gardens containing
more than 200 species of trees and shrubs. In a very
different vein, nearby **Rockingham Motor Speedway**
throbs to the ear-splitting sounds of racing-car engines.
It has 10 different banked track variations, and besides
regular race meetings, the venue also offers visitors
the chance to drive on Europe's fastest circuit – but
it is necessary to book in advance.

⊕
• Take the B670 through
• Cottingham and then turn
• westwards onto the A427
8 into *Market Harborough*.

Travel west to Husbands
Bosworth on the A4304,
then take the A5199 north
and minor roads west to
Ashby Magna. Pick up the
B581 to Barwell then the
A447 north. A minor road
off to the left takes you to
Market Bosworth.

→ • • • • • • • • • • • **9**

8 MARKET HARBOROUGH

Market Harborough began life in the mid 12th century
as a planned market town at a crossing point of the
River Welland. Its original vast market place has been
substantially encroached upon by subsequent building
development, and livestock trading has disappeared
from the town centre, though the original half-timbered
market hall is still *in situ*. The town was King Charles I's
headquarters leading up to the decisive Battle of Naseby
in 1645 (the battle site is six miles to the south east,
in Northamptonshire) and was occupied afterwards
by Cromwell, who used the church as a prison camp.
Along with the usual local history exhibits, **Harborough
Museum** has an interesting corsetry collection donated
by local manufacturer R and W H Symington – in whose
former factory the museum is now housed.

To the west of the town, at **Husbands Bosworth**, there
is a 1,066-m-long (1,166yd) tunnel on the Grand Union
Canal, and a little further north on the same waterway
is **Foxton Locks**, an impressive run of 10 locks that raise
the water level a massive 23m (75ft). The **Foxton Canal
Museum** has fascinating displays of memorabilia, plus
artworks relating to the history of the canals.

9 MARKET BOSWORTH

An unassuming little place, Market Bosworth receives
thousands of visitors each year. Their real destination,
however, is the site of the 1485 Battle of Bosworth,
two miles south of the town. This is where the future
Henry VII, first of the Tudors, triumphed and the
defeated Richard III is supposed to have uttered his
plaintive plea 'a horse, a horse, my kingdom for a
horse'. The **Bosworth Battlefield Visitor Centre** uses
models, displays and interpretative film presentations
to tell the story of the battle. Regular train services,
usually steam-powered, run on the **Battlefield Railway
Line** between here and **Shackerstone**, where there is
a **museum** and a collection of railway rolling stock
and paraphernalia. There are also pretty walks along
the adjacent **Ashby Canal**.

*Head north east, taking
unclassified roads via
Newbold Verdon and Field
Head to **Bradgate Park**.* ⑩

10 BRADGATE PARK

Once a hunting ground within the ancient Charnwood
Forest and still home to a herd of deer, Bradgate Park
is a refreshingly untamed expanse of rough, bracken-
covered parkland punctuated by rabbit warrens, rocky
outcrops and the meandering River Lin. The park's
centrepiece is the ruined **Bradgate House** – whose
most famous inhabitant was Lady Jane Grey, England's
nine-day queen. However, it is equally well known for
one of Leicestershire's most familiar landmarks, the
distinctively shaped tower known as **Old John**. Perched
atop the park's highest hill, the tower was built during
the 18th century, probably as a viewing post for a racecourse that once ringed the hill – although its name is
said to honour a servant who died when a bonfire got
out of control. From here, there are panoramic views
of the surrounding countryside. Bradgate Park also
has a **visitor centre** offering information on the history
of the park, its buildings and its former residents.

*Take unclassified roads
east to East Goscote and
pick up the A607 into
Melton Mowbray.*

← • • • • • • • • • • • • ①

WITH MORE TIME

**Just to the north west of the tour, the Great Central Railway *(left)* operates
Britain's only scheduled mainline steam railway service, between Loughborough
and Leicester. Via a graceful Victorian viaduct, the trains pass over Swithland
Reservoir, host to around 15,000 gulls each winter. Further west, near Ashby-
de-la-Zouch, is Conkers, the hub of a national project to improve our natural
environment by planting more native trees.**

Northamptonshire: squires and spires

Northamptonshire deserves its moniker as 'the county of squires and spires': pretty churches and exquisite manor houses abound, though they now vie for importance with the more modern draws of the county's motor racing circuits. This is primarily an agricultural county, where the rural way of life still holds sway. Sadly, it is little appreciated by the many who speed through on the busy roads and railway lines that connect London with the north of England – but that just means a more peaceful stay for those who do stop to explore the wealth of pretty stone villages and brooding, historic castles that Northamptonshire has to offer.

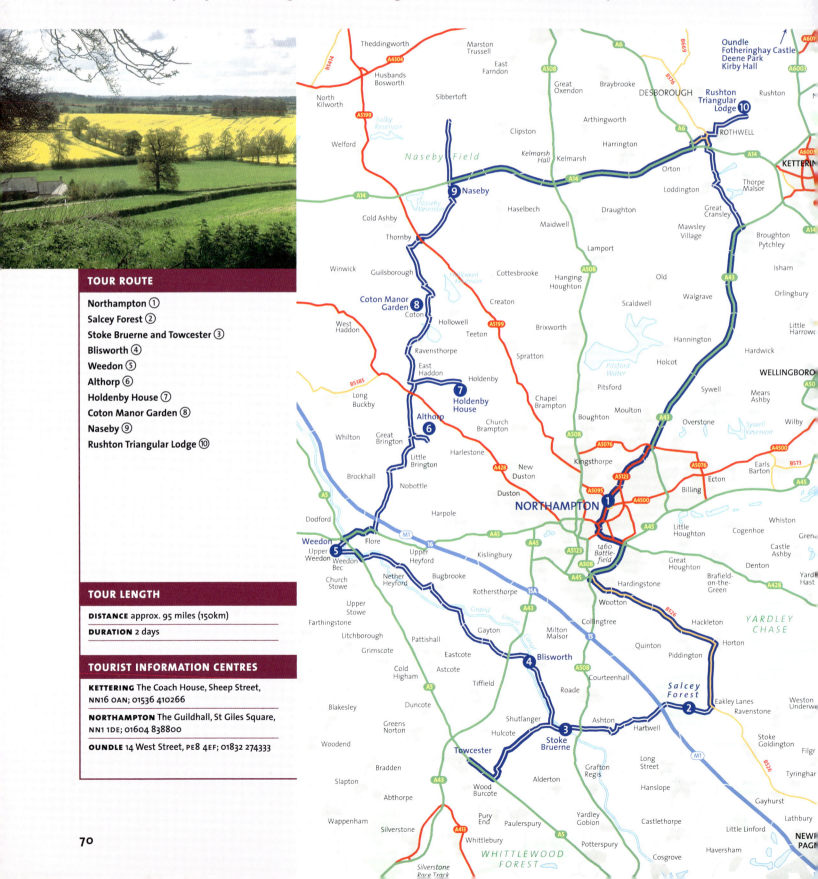

TOUR ROUTE

Northampton ①
Salcey Forest ②
Stoke Bruerne and Towcester ③
Blisworth ④
Weedon ⑤
Althorp ⑥
Holdenby House ⑦
Coton Manor Garden ⑧
Naseby ⑨
Rushton Triangular Lodge ⑩

TOUR LENGTH

DISTANCE approx. 95 miles (150km)

DURATION 2 days

TOURIST INFORMATION CENTRES

KETTERING The Coach House, Sheep Street, NN16 0AN; 01536 410266

NORTHAMPTON The Guildhall, St Giles Square, NN1 1DE; 01604 838800

OUNDLE 14 West Street, PE8 4EF; 01832 274333

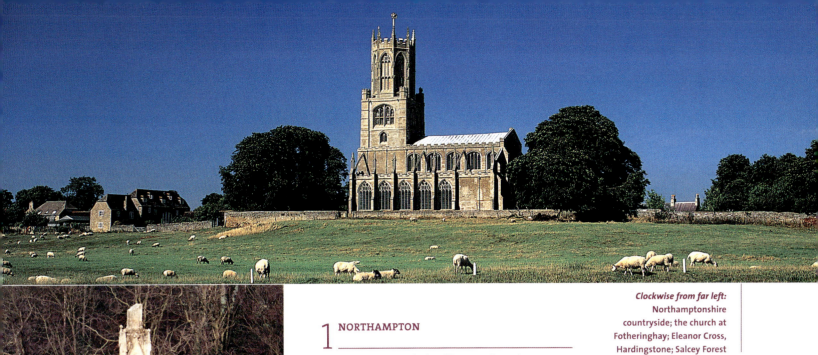

Clockwise from far left:
**Northamptonshire
countryside; the church at
Fotheringhay; Eleanor Cross,
Hardingstone; Salcey Forest**

1 NORTHAMPTON

From riding boots to hobnail boots and simple pumps to high-fashion footwear, Northampton has been shodding the nation's feet since the Middle Ages. At that time, the town's large cattle market and forested outskirts made for easy access to both leather and tanning materials, while Northampton's central location and road, canal and rail links allowed for distribution right across England and, eventually, the world. The aptly named Life and Sole section at **Northampton Museum and Art Gallery** features what is today the world's largest collection of boots and shoes, plus displays that show how such items are produced. There is also an exhibit outlining the history of the town, as well as superb ranges of British art and 15th- to 18th-century Italian paintings. Nearby is the Victorian high Gothic **guildhall**, which contains murals and sculptures by world-renowned artists. **Northampton Castle**, of which only the postern gate survives, is a little further to the west, as is the square-towered **St Peter's Church**, built on Saxon foundations and worth a visit to look at the carvings that remain from that period.

To the south of the town are the site of the 1460 Battle of Northampton and the Eleanor Cross at Hardingstone. This was one of 12 crosses erected between Lincoln and London by Edward I to mark the 12 overnight stops of his wife Eleanor's funeral cortege on the way to Westminster Abbey. It is one of just three originals that can still be seen today. Further west is the 38-ha (95-acre) **Hunsbury Hill Country Park**, the site of an Iron Age hill fort and, later, an ironstone quarry. The railway line that served the quarry is still working, and there is also a small **museum** run by the Northamptonshire Ironstone Railway Trust.

From Northampton, follow signs for the B526 south to Eakley Lanes. Here, turn right and drive on unclassified roads west into Salcey Forest. ②

2 SALCEY FOREST

A haven of peace despite its proximity to the ever-busy M1, Salcey Forest is part of an ancient hunting forest. Some of the oldest trees, known as 'druid oaks', are more than 500 years old and, with their gnarled and sometimes hollow trunks, provide a habitat for a variety of wildlife. There are waymarked hiking routes and a five-mile cycle path, plus a new 'Tree Top Way' that enables you to stroll through the forest canopy.

Continue west on minor roads, crossing the M1 and passing through Hartwell and Ashton to Stoke Bruerne. Drive another 3 miles south west on minor roads and pick up the A5 to reach Towcester.

 • • • • • • • • • • • ③

⤓
*Backtrack to Stoke Bruerne
and take the unclassified
road that runs north along
the canal's eastern bank*
❹ *to get to Blisworth.*

⤓
*Head north west, roughly
following the canal
on unclassified lanes,
to reach Weedon.*
❺

*Take the A45 to Flore, then
turn left towards Little
Brington and Althorp.*
➔ ● ● ● ● ● ● ● ● ● ● ❻

3 STOKE BRUERNE AND TOWCESTER

The tiny canalside village of **Stoke Bruerne** has a pretty
double-span bridge and a cluster of restaurants, pubs
and a tearoom on the waterside. The opening and closing
of the locks always draws a crowd of onlookers, and an
added attraction is the fascinating **canal museum**, set
in an old corn mill and packed with evocative displays
relating to the canals in their commercial heyday. There
are also outdoor exhibits including old working narrow-
boats, plus two pleasant canal walks: a short pedestrian
route to Blisworth Tunnel is on tarmac, or you can follow
the towpath down the flight of seven locks. Short self-
drive cruises on the canal are also available here.

Just to the south of the village, **Stoke Park Pavilions**
features two remarkable 17th-century pavilions and a
grand colonnade, all the work of Inigo Jones. They once
belonged to Stoke Park House, one of the first Palladian
houses in Britain, which burned down in the 1880s. Some
magnificent landscaped gardens with herbaceous
borders and fountains remain, but the majority of the
estate has now been given over to agriculture.

Just to the south west, **Towcester** is a small, attractive
place with a laid-back feel. It was a prosperous coaching
town during the 19th century, and features in Dickens'
The Pickwick Papers, but today it is best known for its
eponymous cheesecake and its fine National Hunt
racecourse. A little further in the same direction is
a rather different kind of racing venue: **Silverstone
Circuit**, most famous as the home of the British Grand
Prix, is a mecca for car and bike enthusiasts. You can
book driving experiences here on non-event days.

4 BLISWORTH

A peaceful and blissfully unspoilt little canalside village,
Blisworth is most renowned for its remarkable 2,800-m-
long tunnel (3,056 yards) – something of an engineering
feat, and the second-longest navigable canal tunnel
in Britain. When entering at one end, only the smallest
pin-prick of light can be seen at the other. In the days
of horse-drawn craft, bargees led their horses over
the hill then returned to 'walk' the barge through the
tunnel by laying on their backs and using their feet
against the ceiling to propel the barge along.

5 WEEDON

Weedon is a little village set astride the Grand Union
Canal, unremarkable were it not for the jumble of
waterside warehouses and other buildings that make
up a giant indoor antiques, bric-a-brac and collectibles
centre run on a semi-cooperative basis by dozens of
individual stallholders. Just to the north, the canal,
the mainline express railway and the M1 motorway
run side by side for several miles through the break
in the hills known as the Watford Gap. The infamous
Gunpowder Plot, which came close to blowing up
King James I and his parliament, was hatched six
miles away, at Ashby St Ledgers.

Clockwise from below:
**the Grand Union Canal,
Stoke Bruerne; Althorp**

6 ALTHORP

The childhood home of Diana, Princess of Wales, Althorp has been owned by the Spencer family for 500 years. It is the epitome of country-house living, having been constantly altered and added to over the years, and its salons contain a remarkable collection of portraiture, including works by Rubens, Reynolds, Van Dyck and Gainsborough, as well as beautiful paintings by many lesser-known artists. The major attraction here, though, is the exhibition 'Diana: A Celebration'; tickets must be bought in advance. Several rooms are devoted to this tribute, which covers everything from Diana's childhood through to the work she did for charity. Profits from ticket sales are donated to her memorial fund.

7 HOLDENBY HOUSE

Close to Althorp stands another of England's great country estates, Holdenby House. Sir Christopher Hatton built a vast mansion here at the end of the 16th century to impress Queen Elizabeth I, but it passed into royal hands when he died not long afterwards. In the years that followed, King James I entertained here and his son, Charles I, was imprisoned here after his defeat in the Battle of Naseby *(see right)*. Set in magnificent gardens that are also home to a falconry centre, Holdenby is now a private home, and is open to the public by appointment.

8 COTON MANOR GARDEN

Tucked away among quiet country lanes near the Ravensthorpe and Hollowell reservoirs is the hillside Coton Manor Garden, laid out by the present owner's grandparents. Each spring, the bluebell-filled woods here are a great attraction, while the series of formal gardens has something in bloom for every season. There is also an attached nursery and a pleasant tearoom.

9 NASEBY

Today a sleepy upland village of attractive red-brick cottages (built by Lord Clifton in the 1870s for his estate workers), Naseby was once the scene of a momentous battle that changed the course of British history. The fierce Battle of Naseby in 1645 marked the turning point in the English Civil War, leading to the royalist army's defeat and the execution of King Charles I. **Cromwell's Table**, one of the best-known landmarks of the Civil War, can be found leaning against the outer wall of All Saints' Church, while the **Battle and Farm Museum** at Purlieu Farm, just outside the village, has an exhibition of weapons used in the battle as well as an impressively detailed reconstruction model.

10 RUSHTON TRIANGULAR LODGE

At Rushton you will find one of England's best-known follies – except it has far deeper significance than a mere rich man's whim. Rushton Triangular Lodge was built by the much-persecuted Sir Thomas Tresham in 1593 as a secretive shrine to his (outlawed) Catholic faith. The theme of the Holy Trinity resonates in all its design features: three walls, three floors, three windows, three gables, and so on, and there are many more religious references besides.

*Head north on unclassified roads to East Haddon, then turn right and follow signs for **Holdenby House**.* **7**

*Backtrack to East Haddon and drive north on minor roads again to reach **Coton Manor Garden**.* **8**

*Drive north, crossing the A5199, and continue north east until you reach **Naseby**.* **9**

*Take the A14 east to Rothwell, then drive north east on unclassified roads to the village of Rushton and **Rushton Triangular Lodge**.* **10**

*Return to Rothwell, cross the A14 and head south on unclassified roads to pick up the A43 back to **Northampton**.*

1

WITH MORE TIME

A hostelry is known to have existed in **Oundle** as far back as AD638, when monks provided sustenance for passing travellers. The town now has many fine inns, a pretty almshouse and the beautiful church of St Peter, with its landmark tower and stained-glass windows. North of Oundle, an earthen mound is all that remains of **Fotheringhay Castle**, where Richard III was born and Mary Queen of Scots was executed, while to the west, towards Corby, are **Deene Park** and **Kirby Hall** *(left)* – two fine manor houses. The latter is little more than a shell, but reeks of atmosphere.

Berkshire, Oxfordshire, Buckinghamshire and Gloucestershire

Windsor and the royal reaches of the Thames

This stretch of countryside, between the gently undulating Chiltern Hills to the north and the twisting and curving Thames to the south, has been home to royalty for centuries. It's easy to see why: just a few miles from the built-up London suburbs, you'll find tiny, unspoilt villages, wooded areas, country lanes and breathtaking scenery, along with a mood of peace and tranquility that is truly rare this close to the capital.

TOUR ROUTE

Windsor ①
Runnymede ②
Eton College ③
Stoke Poges ④
Burnham Beeches ⑤
Cliveden ⑥
West Wycombe ⑦
Hughenden Manor ⑧
Marlow ⑨
Hambleden ⑩

TOUR LENGTH

DISTANCE approx. 70 miles (110km)

DURATION 3 days

TOURIST INFORMATION CENTRES

HIGH WYCOMBE Paul's Row, HP11 2HQ;
01494 421892

MARLOW 31 High Street, SL7 1AU; 01628 483597

WINDSOR 24 High Street, SL4 1LH; 01753 743900

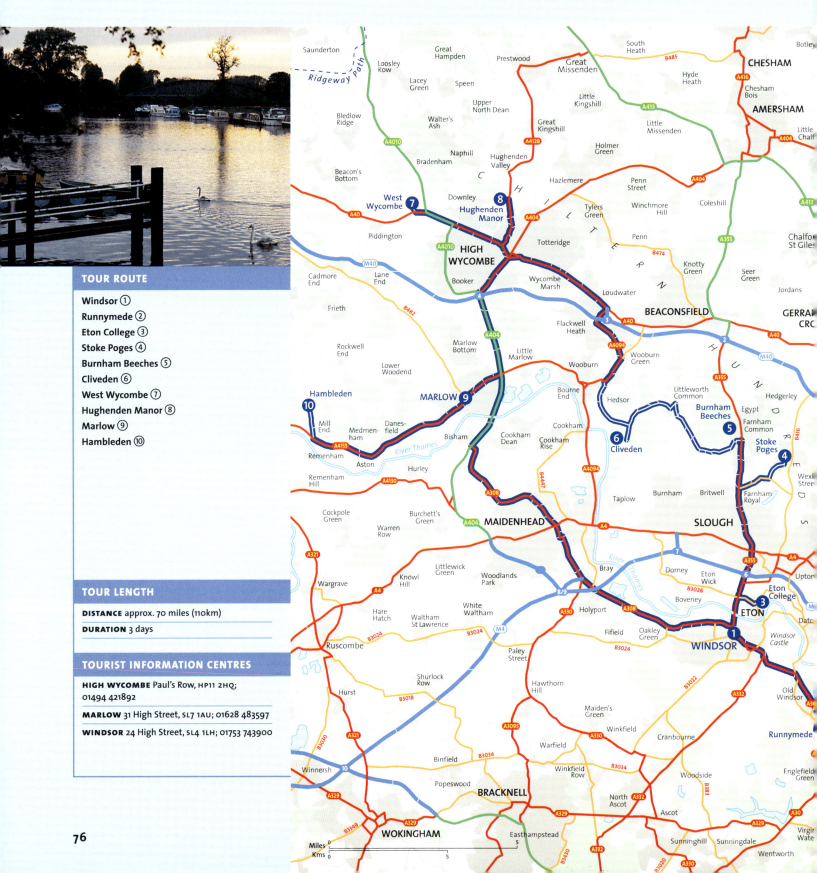

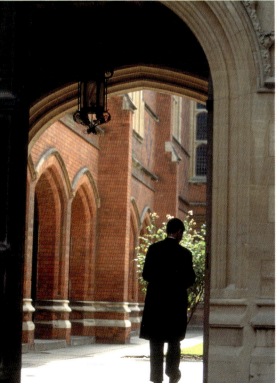

Clockwise from far left:
the River Thames at
Windsor; view of Windsor
Castle; guards at Windsor
Castle; Eton College

1 WINDSOR

The seat of England's royalty for more than 900 years, **Windsor Castle** is without a doubt the main reason for visiting the town. Towering over the nearby river and the pretty buildings that cluster beneath its soaring battlements, it is as imposing as such a venerable royal residence should be. The State Apartments do not disappoint, combining furnishings and tapestries of unrivalled sumptuousness with an extraordinary collection of priceless and historically significant paintings. There are works by Rembrandt, Rubens, Canaletto and Gainsborough, plus the famous triple portrait of Charles I by Van Dyck. The 14th-century St George's Chapel is the most lavish example of Gothic architecture in England and holds the tombs of ten sovereigns, among them Henry VIII (and his third wife Jane Seymour) and Charles I.

Just to the south, the 2,000-ha (5,000-acre) **Windsor Great Park** extends further than the eye can see. It's a wonderful space for a stroll down long avenues of trees and past herds of deer. In the park's south-east section lies the horticulturally diverse **Savill Garden**, stocked with an array of plants that ensure a colourful display year round. On the other side of the castle lies the busy riverfront, edged with meadows and dotted with occasional pubs and restaurants.

*Head south east out of Windsor on the A308, turn right onto the A328 after Old Windsor and look out for the signs on the left to **Runnymede**.* **2**

2 RUNNYMEDE

The riverside meadows, woods and rich flora in this area make it an attractive enough spot to visit, but Runnymede is also a site of historical significance. This is where King John signed the Magna Carta in 1215, agreeing to enshrine and be bound by certain laws of the land, and thus beginning a process that eventually evolved into the rule of constitutional law. It is commemorated in a pleasing woodland glade with a monument erected by the American Bar Association in 1957 (in celebration of the link between the Magna Carta and the US Constitution). There is also a John F Kennedy memorial nearby, and on the opposite bank of the Thames stands the venerable **Ankerwycke Yew**, thought to be more than 2,000 years old.

*Return to Windsor and cross the Thames on the A355, turning right onto the B3026 and then following the signs for **Eton College**.*

 **3**

Clockwise from above:
Burnham Beeches; Cliveden;
Cliveden interior; street,
West Wycombe

⬇ Head back to the A355
   northbound, and turn right
   onto Park Road at Farnham
   Royal, then left onto the
④ minor road into **Stoke Poges**.

⬇ Return to the A355 and
   continue north for less
   than 2 miles. Look out for
   the sign for **Burnham
   Beeches** and its car park
⑤ on the left.

ASCOT

Just south west of Windsor Great Park, Ascot racecourse is a wonderfully atmospheric venue popular with serious horseracing fans as well as those who just like to have a flutter. Founded in 1711 by Queen Anne, who spotted the potential of this patch of land while out riding, Ascot was laid out as a course 'for horses to gallop at full stretch'. Almost 300 years later, it is still a major venue for flat and National Hunt racing, staging 27 of the most celebrated and keenly competed days in the racing calendar. Among them is the three-day Ascot Festival, a prestigious competition that pits some of the world's top thoroughbreds against each other over the flat.

The course is perhaps best known, however, for its Royal Ascot meeting in June. This is as much a social occasion as a sporting one, where for many visitors style – especially the hats – and people-watching seem almost to eclipse the excitement of the races themselves.

3 ETON COLLEGE

Boarding school to the wealthy, the well-connected and the privileged, including princes William and Harry, Eton has a long and illustrious history that dates back to 1440. Rather like a visit to one of the older Oxbridge colleges, a tour of these ancient halls and brick-walled courtyards conveys a compelling sense of centuries of tradition mingling with the everyday lives of the current students.

4 STOKE POGES

Just far enough away to escape the sprawl of busy Slough, Stoke Poges is a pretty hamlet surrounded by pleasingly meandering country lanes. Apart from the air of relaxed calm, the main attraction is **St Giles Church** – resting place of the poet Thomas Gray, who is most famous for his 'Elegy Written in a Country Churchyard'. St Giles is also said to have been the inspiration for the elegy, and to this day you can still feel the sense of stillness and calm Gray evokes in his elegant meditation on mortality and ambition. The church dates back to Saxon times, although there are Norman, Gothic and Tudor elements. Look out for the large, squat memorial to the poet.

5 BURNHAM BEECHES

Mentioned in the Domesday Book, and cultivated and managed continuously ever since, this 220-ha (540-acre) patch of beech wood, heath and meadow scattered with streams and ponds is a delight to explore. Hugely popular, it attracts 500,000 visitors a year – but this press of visitors is seldom apparent. There are several well-signposted, self-guided walks around the various paths and habitats, which are home to a diverse range of flora and fauna including fungi and rare bats. Autumn is, of course, the most spectacular season, but this is a magical destination for a ramble at any time of year.

6 CLIVEDEN

Stroll the banks of the Thames west of London for any distance and you'll catch tantalising glimpses of grand riverside mansions. Not all are open to the public, but you can explore the most spectacular one: Grade I-listed Cliveden. The gardens are captivatingly romantic, featuring lovingly crafted topiary, statues, water gardens, woods and riverside walks. Even against this backdrop, the Italianate house is palatial: the oak-panelled Great Hall, complete with an ornate 16th-century stone fireplace, tapestries and a suit of armour, sets the tone. Built by Charles Barry for the Duke of Sutherland in 1851, Cliveden was latterly the home of glamorous socialite Lady Astor and her set of famous and often controversial friends – including John Profumo, who met showgirl Christine Keeler here in 1961 while he was Secretary of State for War and she was having an affair with a Russian naval attaché. The resulting scandal was serious enough to bring down the government of Prime Minister Harold MacMillan. Cliveden is not open every day, so check before you visit.

7 WEST WYCOMBE

A pretty, typically Chiltern village, West Wycombe is synonymous with Sir Francis Dashwood, a hell-raising 18th-century baronet who in his quieter moments oversaw the construction of the house and landscaping of the estate at **West Wycombe Park**. Considered the best example of Palladian architecture in England, and filled with fine painted ceilings, pictures, furniture and sculpture, the house remains the home of the Dashwood family today. Outdoor attractions include statues, grottoes and an ornamental lake. Dashwood famously founded the Hellfire Club, a society of louche aristocrats who liked to drink and gamble, which convened in caves beneath the ancestral church of St Lawrence nearby, and where all sorts of erotic and blasphemous goings on have been rumoured and conjectured. The **Hell Fire Caves** are open for viewing.

Skirt south of Burnham Beeches on unclassified roads, continuing north west to Littleworth Common and then roughly west, following the signs for Cliveden. **6**

Backtrack less than 1 mile before turning left towards Bourne End. Pick up the A4094 north, crossing the M40, and then take the A40 west through High Wycombe to West Wycombe. **7**

Return to the centre of High Wycombe on the A40, turn left onto the A4128 and look out for the signs to Hughenden Manor just off the road on the left, about 1 mile from High Wycombe.

8

Clockwise from above:
street, Marlow; riverside,
Marlow; mill, Hambleden;
Hughenden Manor

*Head back into High
Wycombe again, and then
south on the A404. Turn
west on the A4155 into
the centre of Marlow.*

 • • • • • • • • • • • ⑨

8 HUGHENDEN MANOR

Hughenden's chief attraction is its superbly preserved
interior, richly redolent of its heyday during the prime
ministership of Benjamin Disraeli, who lived here
from 1848 until 1881. The walls are lined with portraits
and documents from that era, and Disraeli's study
has been left much as it was at the time when he
managed the affairs of state and empire from here.
There's also an interesting new exhibition on the
secret role Hughenden played as a nerve centre for
the UK's hugely successful code-breaking operations
during World War II. The rather severe Gothic brick
exterior may not be to all tastes, but the formal
gardens provide an enjoyable setting for a stroll.

THE CHILTERN HILLS

The beech woods and flint-faced hamlets of
the Chilterns have long been favourite retreats
of celebrities, politicians and London commuters
alike. Much of the region is rightly designated
an Area of Outstanding Natural Beauty.
Prehistoric pathways thread through this part
of the country, forming a rough highway that
once ran almost from the south coast, through
the Chilterns and, along the possibly even
more ancient Icknield Way, as far as Norfolk.
Wendover is a good starting point for walks
in the area – or you can take in the amazing
scenery from the comfort of a steam train on
the **Chinnor and Princes Risborough Railway**
(open weekends from spring to autumn).

10 HAMBLEDEN

This tiny village in a glorious Chiltern setting is an improbably pretty cluster of brick and flint cottages, set around a perfectly preserved village square complete with a village pump, a chestnut tree and a church. There's also an atmospheric pub and a village store and delicatessen. According to the Domesday Book, the settlement dates back at least as far as the 11th century. The village sits in a 650-ha (1,600-acre) estate of beech woodlands and rolling fields, with an avenue of lime trees. Unsurprisingly, Hambleden has appeared in a whole host of feature films and TV shows including *Chitty Chitty Bang Bang*, *Sleepy Hollow*, *Poirot* and *Rosemary and Thyme*.

Continue south west along the A4155, turn right at Mill End and follow the lane into **Hambleden**. 10

Return through Marlow to the A404, driving south to join the A308 through Maidenhead and back into **Windsor**.

← • • • • • • • • • • 1

9 MARLOW

There's no one single attraction to compel a visit to Marlow. It is simply a charmingly situated town offering a mix of riverside walks, an elegant suspension bridge, several fine Georgian buildings, appealing pubs, and an attractive backdrop of wooded countryside. Marlow also has numerous literary associations: Percy Byssche and Mary Shelley, T S Eliot and Jerome K Jerome have all lived or stayed here over the years. During summertime, Salter's Steamers runs pleasure-boat trips from here to Henley, Windsor and Maidenhead.

WITH MORE TIME

Walking the 85-mile **Ridgeway Path** *(left)* – which starts just north of Tring, passes a number of Neolithic sites and burial mounds and ends at Avebury's mysterious stone circles – is a wonderful way to get a feel for this part of the country and its prehistoric past. It's easy to park the car and pick up the Ridgeway at key points along its journey, which takes in or passes close to several delightful Chiltern villages – including Princes Risborough and Chinnor.

Oxford: city of dreaming spires and beyond

World-renowned for its architecture, museums and elite academic record, Oxford is, for many visitors, synonymous with Oxfordshire. But venture past the honey-coloured buildings into the rambling lanes and out to the surrounding countryside and you'll find an entire county steeped in history and tradition. Combining rolling hills with manicured lawns, stately homes and pretty villages, Oxfordshire is the perfect rural retreat.

TOUR ROUTE

Oxford ①
Abingdon ②
Wantage ③
Didcot Railway Centre ④
Wallingford ⑤
Goring ⑥
Beale Park ⑦
Mapledurham House and Mill ⑧
Henley-on-Thames ⑨
Stonor Park ⑩
Watlington ⑪

TOUR LENGTH

DISTANCE approx. 90 miles (145km)
DURATION 2–3 days

TOURIST INFORMATION CENTRES

DIDCOT 118 Broadway, OX11 8AB; 01235 813243

HENLEY ON THAMES King's Arms Bar, Kings Road, RG9 2DG; 01491 578034

OXFORD 15/16 Broad Street, OX1 3AS; 01865 726871

WALLINGFORD Town Hall, Market Place, OX10 0EG; 01491 826972

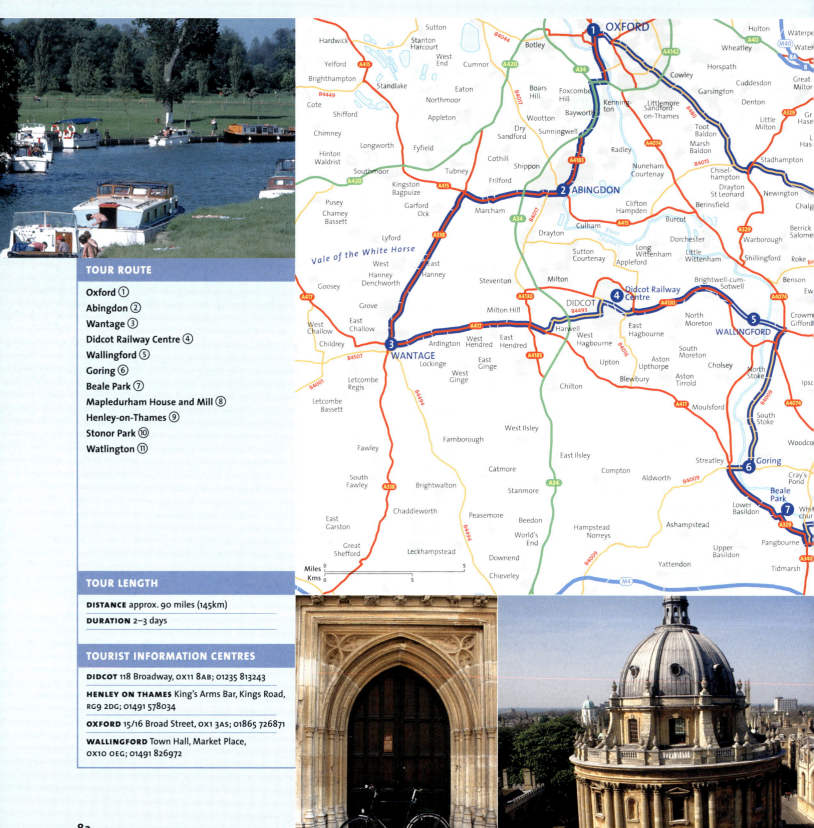

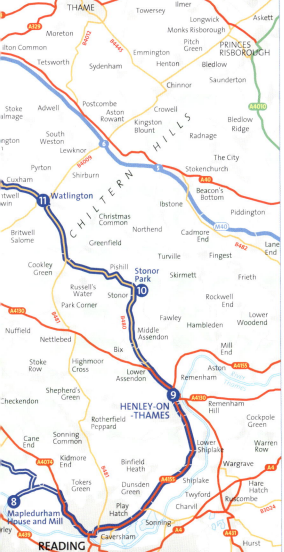

Clockwise from far left:
Abingdon; Oxford city and
university skyline; punting
on the River Isis; Radcliffe
Camera, Oxford; entrance to
Merton College, Oxford

1 OXFORD

The city of dreaming spires has been known over the years as everything from a marriage market for the rich to the birthplace of the Morris Minor, but most visitors still come here for the university. The city centre is full of gorgeous old colleges *(see p84)*, many of which are open to the public at various times of day. Outside these hours, you may still catch a tantalising glimpse through the heavy old doors to the ivy-clad quads beyond.

Many of Oxford's historic buildings are connected to the university in one way or another. Probably the most famous landmark of all is the **Radcliffe Camera**, a stunning Italianate rotunda that now houses part of the collection from the **Bodleian Library**. The Bodleian is one of oldest libraries in the world, and still a place reserved for serious academic study – but guided tours take visitors through such highlights as the incredible Gothic Jacobean courtyard and the impressive 15th-century Divinity School with its intricate vaulted ceiling. Next door, the **Sheldonian Theatre**, Sir Christopher Wren's first major work, was created while he was professor of astronomy at the university. It has a superb painted ceiling and is regularly used for concerts and recitals.

Oxford is also home to the **Ashmolean Museum** with its grand classical façade and vast collection. It is Britain's oldest public museum and has everything from Egyptian mummies and classical art to Islamic, Chinese and French masterpieces and assemblages of porcelain and silver-ware. For something on a more manageable scale try the **Oxford University Museum of Natural History**, which is stuffed with fascinating finds and housed in a stunning Victorian Gothic building featuring cast iron columns and a glass roof. To the back is the captivating **Pitt Rivers Museum**, a treasure chest of feathered cloaks, shrunken heads, blowpipes and mummies.

If you visit in summer, make sure to leave enough time to enjoy the quintessential Oxford experience: punting on the Isis (as the River Thames is known here). Stop at the traditional covered market for picnic supplies, grab a bottle of Pimms and then attempt to glide gracefully down the river. Alternatively, try one of the many Oxford guided walks for an insight into the city's past, its literary connections or even the favourite haunts of Inspector Morse.

*From Oxford, follow
signs to the A34, driving
south to pick up the
A4183 into* **Abingdon**.

STICKLERS FOR TRADITION

The Oxford colleges are well known for their weird and wonderful traditions. One of the most beautiful is celebrated at dawn on May Day morning when the Magdalen College choristers sing madrigals from the top of the church tower. More bizarrely, Merton College students have been known to walk backwards around their quad for an hour at 2am on the night the clocks go back to settle a philosophical debate over the missing hour. Time is also of the essence at Christ Church, where at 9.05pm each evening the bells of Tom Tower ring out 101 times to sound the curfew for the original 101 scholars. Why 9.05? Because Oxford is five minutes and two seconds behind Greenwich Mean Time. At Lincoln College, academics and choristers celebrate Ascension Day by 'beating the bounds' of St Michael's Parish. However, the parish boundaries now cut through Marks and Spencers and Boots so look out for singing men wielding sticks while you are stocking up on essentials. After traipsing around the parish grounds, the group then throws hot pennies from the college tower to waiting school children below – supposedly to teach them a lesson about the evil of greed.

OXFORD'S COLLEGES

Oxford University is made up of 39 separate colleges, the oldest of which date from the 13th century; each has its own character and speciality. One of the most popular colleges with visitors is **Christ Church**, home to the city's only cathedral and *alma mater* to Einstein and no fewer than 13 British prime ministers. To one side of the enormous quad, a set of stone steps, featured in the *Harry Potter* films, leads to the spectacular refectory where Lewis Carroll is said to have eaten 8,000 meals. By contrast, **Magdalen** is smaller and more intimate, with a beautiful medieval chapel and bell tower, and secluded cloisters surrounded by figures that inspired C S Lewis's characters in *The Chronicles of Narnia*. This is the wealthiest of Oxford's colleges and its extensive grounds and deer park are wonderful for walking. **Merton College**, founded in 1264, is one of the oldest in Oxford and has a stunning medieval library, while **Brasenose** and **New College** are also charming colleges worth visiting.

Take the A415 west to join the A338, and then proceed south to **Wantage**.

2 ABINGDON

The elegant market town of Abingdon has a pretty riverside setting and a clutch of distinctive buildings. Little remains of the town's famous abbey, which was once larger than Westminster's, so pride of place in the architectural stakes now goes to the grand County Hall, built by one of Wren's master masons. Inside, the **Abingdon Museum** gives a good insight into the town's history. A short stroll away is the late-15th-century **Merchant's Hall** with its beautiful wall paintings and windows, and at the end of the same street you'll find the Perpendicular-style **St Helen's Church** – boasting a glorious 14th-century painted roof – as well as a group of picturesque 15th-century almshouses.

3 WANTAGE

The attractive but unassuming town of Wantage was an important Saxon centre and birthplace of the most beloved of English kings, Alfred the Great, in AD849. His statue now adorns the town square, which is flanked by handsome Georgian and Victorian buildings interspersed with narrow cobbled streets and lanes. The **Vale and Downland Museum** has interesting displays on local history and geology and is a good place to plan a walking tour on the nearby **Ridgeway Path** *(see p81)*.

4 DIDCOT RAILWAY CENTRE

A mecca for train lovers, the Didcot Railway Centre features a host of Great Western Railway steam engines, a lovingly restored country station and an old engine shed full of treasures. The trains are fired up on regular steam days when passengers can enjoy old-style travel and learn about postal trains and Victorian signalling.

5 WALLINGFORD

Founded by Alfred the Great, the handsome market town of Wallingford reveals traces of its Saxon walls even today. The elegant riverside church, sturdy town hall and local museum are well worth a visit, while across the river are the remains of an 11th-century castle and mint. From Wallingford you can hop on the Cholsey and Wallingford Steam Railway west to village of **Cholsey**, where crime-writer Agatha Christie is buried.

6 GORING

Nestled between the Chilterns and the Berkshire Downs, the picturesque town of Goring is home to an array of pretty, traditional shops, stone houses, half-timbered buildings and a lovely Norman church. Surrounded by the most dramatic scenery on the Thames, it is an excellent base for walking tours in the nearby hills.

*Drive east on the A417 and then turn north east onto the B4493 into Didcot for the **Didcot Railwway Centre**.* **4**

*Continue east on the A4130, taking minor roads for the last mile into **Wallingford**.* **5**

*Drive east out of town and take the A4074 south, picking up the B4009 at Crowmarsh Gifford to reach **Goring**.* **6**

*Head south on the A329 and look out for the turning for **Beale Park** on the left.*

 7

⊕ *Continue south on the A329 and turn left onto the B471 to Whitchurch. Turn right in the village and right again at the next crossroads, then follow the* **8** *signs for* **Mapledurham**.

7 BEALE PARK

Enjoying a beautiful location within an Area of Outstanding Natural Beauty, Beale Park is a 120-ha (300-acre) organic water meadow and wildlife reserve that is managed in traditional ways. The park boasts a collection of rare breed farm animals, but the main attraction is the bird collection, which includes everything from peacocks and parrots to flamingos and owls. There's also a deer park, with plenty of pleasant walks and picnic spots throughout the grounds.

⊕ *Head east to join the A4074, travelling south on this road until the junction with the A4155, which will take you* **9** *north east to* **Henley**.

8 MAPLEDURHAM HOUSE AND MILL

A long, narrow, twisting lane leads to Mapledurham, a tiny estate village unspoilt by modern life. The imposing red-brick pile here was home to the Blount family for more than 500 years and a refuge for Catholics during the Reformation. Developed from a 12th-century manor house, the building was much enlarged in Elizabethan times and altered again in the 18th and 19th centuries. Fine plasterwork, giant oak staircases and a collection of portraits and furniture adorn the family rooms, as well as an array of personal possessions bequeathed to Martha Blount by 18th-century poet Alexander Pope. There's also a gorgeous chapel in early Gothic revival style and a 15th-century water mill restored to full working order – the last of its kind on the Thames.

9 HENLEY-ON-THAMES

Elegant, affluent Henley-on-Thames is most famous for its July regatta, which sees the best amateur rowers in the world thrashing it out on the River Thames, just as they have done since 1839. The races, however, can seem little more than a sideshow to the real business of picnicking, quaffing champagne, and gossiping in the spectators' enclosure. For the rest of the year, Henley is a sleepy place where Georgian townhouses, chi-chi shops and a clutch of Tudor buildings line the streets. On the main drag, Hart Street, the stocky **St Mary's Church** is also worth a look, if only to visit the grave of Dusty Springfield. Down on the river banks, the **River and Rowing Museum** does a great job of explaining the town's history and its connections to the rowing world, or you could opt to take a boat tour from here to get a first-hand glimpse of the river at work.

Drive north on the A4130 and turn right onto the B480 to reach **Stonor Park**.

→ • • • • • • • • • • • **10**

Clockwise from far left:
regatta, Henley-on-Thames;
Mapledurham House;
Stonor House; Watlington
Hill; regatta attendee,
Henley-on-Thames

10 STONOR PARK

Set in a delightfully secluded fold of the Chiltern Hills
(see p80), this estate – the home of the Stonor family
for more than 800 years – has an impressive array of
buildings that blend medieval, Tudor, Georgian and
Gothic styles. Long a centre of Catholicism, in 1581
Stonor Park offered refuge to St Edmund Campion,
a Jesuit priest, and the room he used now features a
small exhibition on his life and work. Elsewhere, there
are fine collections of family portraits, Italian art and
bronzes, silhouettes and ceramics, while the medieval
chapel contains Stations of the Cross carved during
World War II by a Polish prisoner of war and donated
by author Graham Greene. Outside, there are walled
hillside gardens and a deer park.

Head north again on
the B480 for 8 miles
*to **Watlington**.* ⓫

11 WATLINGTON

Nestled at the foot of the Chilterns, Watlington is the
smallest market town in England, and it has a pretty
17th-century town hall built by Thomas Stonor. Isolated
from the canals and the railways, the town never boomed,
so its historic core remains largely intact. Although
many of the medieval buildings were altered during
the 18th and 19th centuries, Watlington still holds a
certain charm and is designated a conservation area.

Continue north west
along the B480 to
*return to **Oxford**.*
← • • • • • • • • • • • • ①

WITH MORE TIME

The most obvious of the ancient sites in the **Vale of the White Horse** is the giant,
stylised white horse itself *(left)* – thought to be one of Britain's oldest hill carvings.
No one is sure when or why it was created, but it might commemorate King Alfred's
victory in the Battle of Ashdown, or even be a sacred site. Massive earthworks on
top of the hill mark the spot of Bronze Age Uffington Castle. Nearby, flat-topped
Dragon's Hill is hailed as the place where St George slew the dragon: a bare patch
here is supposedly where the beast's blood fell, killing off the grass.

The Cherwell Valley and the Vale of Aylesbury: a retreat of millionaires

The idle rich have been attracted by the lush countryside and rolling hills of Buckinghamshire and Oxfordshire for centuries, and they have left behind an unprecedented legacy of stately homes. This playground of millionaires and exiles has lured everyone from royalty to banking magnates, and with them the best of Britain's architects and landscape gardeners.

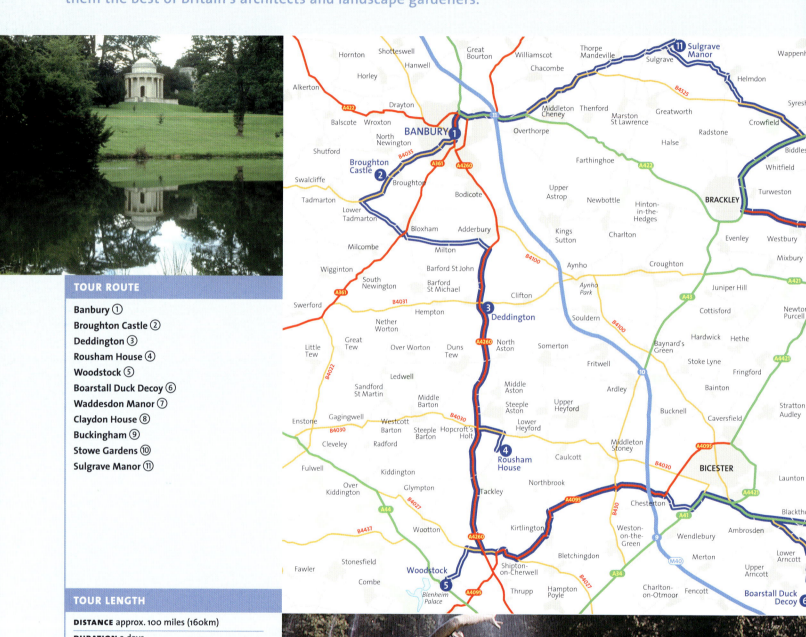

TOUR ROUTE

Banbury ①
Broughton Castle ②
Deddington ③
Rousham House ④
Woodstock ⑤
Boarstall Duck Decoy ⑥
Waddesdon Manor ⑦
Claydon House ⑧
Buckingham ⑨
Stowe Gardens ⑩
Sulgrave Manor ⑪

TOUR LENGTH

DISTANCE approx. 100 miles (160km)

DURATION 3 days

TOURIST INFORMATION CENTRES

BANBURY Spiceball Park Road, ox16 2PQ;
01295 259855

BUCKINGHAM The Old Gaol Museum, Market Hill,
MK18 1JX; 01280 823020

WOODSTOCK Oxfordshire Museum, Park Street,
ox20 1SN; 01993 813276

Clockwise from far left:
Stowe gardens; Broughton
Castle; Claydon House;
fountain, Waddeson Manor

1 BANBURY

An ancient market town that grew rich from the wool trade in medieval times, Banbury is a workaday place with a charming old core. At the centre is the latest, 19th-century incarnation of the Banbury Cross, made famous by the nursery rhyme Ride a Cock Horse – and close by, on South Bar, a bronze statue depicts the 'fyne lady upon a white horse'. Banbury was ravaged by fire in 1628, and many of the elegant buildings around the town today date from that time. The **Banbury Museum** has displays on the history of the town and encompasses Tooley's Boatyard, which has been in continuous use since 1778.

Drive south west from
Banbury on the B4035 to
get to Broughton and
follow the signs for
Broughton Castle. ②

2 BROUGHTON CASTLE

Surrounded by gentle sloping hills and often clouded in mist, fairy-tale Broughton Castle is more manor house than true castle, but it is still an incredibly romantic and atmospheric place that cannot fail to make an impression. The moated medieval building has its own 14th-century church and is set in extensive grounds. It is home to Lord Saye and Sele, but opens to the public on certain days. The castle is a favourite with film location scouts and featured in both *Shakespeare in Love* and *The Madness of King George*.

Continue south on the
B4035 and turn left
towards Bloxham.
Drive through Milton
to join the A4260
south to Deddington. ③

3 DEDDINGTON

The sleepy market village of Deddington is a gracious place with a host of fine houses and buildings dating right back to the Middle Ages. Half-timbered inns, almshouses, antique shops and picturesque cottages of honey-coloured stone line the village streets, and on the main street there's a medieval hall house. In addition, there's neoclassical **Deddington Manor**, the gorgeous **Castle House**, which is built on the foundations of a 13th-century tower-like structure, and – near the grassy mounds that mark the spot of 12th-century Deddington Castle – **Castle End** is a lovely medieval hall with a gabled doorway.

Drive south along the
A4260 to Hopcrofts Holt,
then turn left along the
B4030 and follow the signs
for Rousham House.
④

OTMOOR RSPB RESERVE

Crisscrossed by a labyrinth of paths, Otmoor is an unexpected stretch of marshy wilderness surrounded by seven historic villages. Made up of reedbeds and meadows, the moor is a haven for thousands of birds and provides a breeding habitat for many species. The area is protected as a nature reserve and makes a great spot for some leisurely walking; however, parts of the moor are used as an army firing range, so be sure to check all notices and do not enter the marked areas if red flags are flying.

4 ROUSHAM HOUSE

Rousham House is a wonderful Jacobean pile built by Sir Robert Dormer in the 17th century and owned by the same family ever since. The house manages to preserve the spirit of the era without even a hint of commercialism and makes a fantastic place to wander and just soak up the atmosphere. The main draw here, however, is William Kent's fabulous gardens, almost unaltered since he laid them out in the 18th century. Classical statues, temples, terraces and water features adorn the trails, and a folly designed as a ruin still stands in the grounds.

Backtrack to the A4260 and drive south to the junction with the B4027, turning right and then left onto the unclassified road to Woodstock.

 ● ● ● ● ● ● ● ● ● ● ● 5

Clockwise from far left:
interior at Blenheim Palace,
Woodstock; Boarstall Tower;
Blenheim Palace, Woodstock

5 WOODSTOCK

The beautiful, honey-coloured village of Woodstock
has been a favoured haunt of royalty since Saxon times
and boasts a wonderful collection of buildings around
the market square. The town hall and village church
are worth a look, and the **Oxfordshire Museum** does
an excellent job of explaining the history of the area.
The main attraction here, however, is **Blenheim Palace**,
an extravagant Italianate pile that has been home
to the Churchill family since the 18th century. Queen
Anne awarded John Churchill, Duke of Marlborough,
the Woodstock estate and enough cash to build this
extraordinary home after his victory over the French
at the Battle of Blenheim in 1704. The house was
designed by Sir John Vanbrugh with some additional
work by Nicholas Hawksmoor, and is crammed with
paintings, antiques, porcelain and tapestries as well as
an exhibition on Sir Winston Churchill, who was born
here and is buried at nearby **Bladon Church**. The house
can get incredibly busy, but the vast landscaped
grounds make a wonderful escape from the crowds.

6 BOARSTALL DUCK DECOY

Dating from the 17th century, the duck decoy at Boarstall
is one of only a handful of working decoys remaining
in England. Owned by the National Trust, which keeps a
fully-trained decoy dog and offers regular demonstrations
to visitors in season, the site was once used to trap
wildfowl for food, but the birds caught here today are
ringed by ornithologists before being set free. The
site is now a nature reserve, with walking trails and
an interesting visitor centre. The rather imposing,
crenellated **Boarstall Tower**, on the same site, was
once the gatehouse of the 14th-century Boarstall
House, and is now all that remains of it.

*Return to the B4027 and
drive east, picking up
the A4095 to Chesterton
and then cutting across to
the south of Bicester on the
A41. After 2.5 miles, turn
south on the B4011 to reach
the Boarstall Duck Decoy.* **6**

*Backtrack to the A41 and
drive east to Waddesdon,
following signs for
Waddesdon Manor.*
7

8 CLAYDON HOUSE

Hidden behind a rather sober neoclassical façade, the sumptuous interiors of Claydon House are a masterpiece of rococo style. Originally a Jacobean house, Claydon was remodelled in the 1750s when the latest craze was Chinoiserie. Intricate wood carvings adorn the incredible Chinese room, delicate plasterwork blankets the ceilings and the spectacular parquetry staircase is worked from mahogany, ebony and ivory. The house was occupied by the Verney family for over 380 years and their relative, Florence Nightingale, was a regular visitor. Many of her personal mementoes are on display here.

9 BUCKINGHAM

Nestled in a bend on the River Ouse, the unassuming market town of Buckingham was the county capital until the 16th century, though it was almost destroyed by fire in 1725. The town was rebuilt in model Georgian style and is now a bustling place with the wide, sloping Market Hill running down to the castle-like **Old Gaol**. This now houses the tourist information centre and a modest local museum. Buckingham's oldest building, however, is the mostly 15th-century **Buckingham Chantry Chapel**, first used as a hospital and still sporting its Norman arch. Also worth a look is the hilltop church of St Peter and St Paul. Marked trails follow the Ouse towpath and offer gentle walks in both directions.

Follow minor roads north via Quainton and East Claydon to Middle Claydon **8** *and* **Claydon House.**

Drive north again on unclassified roads, through Padbury and onto the A413 **9** *north into* **Buckingham.**

Head west on the A422 and follow the signs to **Stowe Gardens.**

→ • • • • • • • • • • • **10**

7 WADDESDON MANOR

All the ostentatious wealth and Victorian exuberance of Baron Ferdinand Rothschild is on display at his extravagant mansion just outside Aylesbury. Completed in 1889, the hilltop French chateau is a testimony to his opulent taste and massive wealth. The house was never intended as a residence but was used to entertain select guests and is stuffed full of Savonnerie carpets, Sèvres porcelain, French furniture, and paintings by Gainsborough and Reynolds. All together they make up one of the most important collections of 18th-century decorative arts in the world. Outside, the recently restored gardens are one of the finest examples of 19th-century landscaping in Britain, complete with a rococo revival aviary.

Clockwise from far left:
Waddeson Manor; Palladian
bridge, Stowe Gardens;
Chinese-style painting,
Claydon House

10 STOWE GARDENS

Hidden away down a long, tree-lined driveway, the elite **Stowe School** occupies a palatial house that is open to the public outside term times. It is surrounded by the stunning National Trust-run Stowe Gardens: over the years a series of wealthy families lived here and employed the best gardeners of their time, including Sir John Vanbrugh, James Gibbs, William Kent, and 'Capability' Brown. Between them, they created one of the most influential landscape gardens in Europe. The 101-ha (250-acre) grounds feature a Palladian bridge, ornamental lakes and more than 40 monuments, sculptures and decorative features.

11 SULGRAVE MANOR

The compact Tudor manor house at Sulgrave is the ancestral home of the Washingtons in Britain, and was bought by Lawrence Washington in the mid 16th-century. George Washington never came here but the family coat of arms, which includes stars and stripes, can be seen above the arches in the doorway and in the great hall and may even have been the inspiration for the American flag. The house contains a collection of George Washington memorabilia, but is worth a visit in its own right for a look at the mighty great hall, the oak panelled 18th-century parlour, the 200-year-old kitchen implements and the Queen Anne white and chintz bedrooms. Outside there's a knot garden plus the National Herb Garden, which showcases herbs used in Tudor times.

*Return to the A422 west,
turning north at the
junction with the A43.
Turn left onto the B4525
and follow the signs
for Sulgrave Manor.* **11**

*Continue west on minor
roads, picking up the B4525
again and driving south
west onto the A422 to
return to Banbury.*

WITH MORE TIME

The original Jacobean house at Ascott was acquired by the super-rich Baron Mayer de Rothschild in the 19th century, and as it was passed down the family line, the house was substantially altered. Today, the house is the showcase for an extraordinary and expansive collection of paintings, fine French and English furniture and one of the most important collections of oriental porcelain in the world. Outside, the wonderful gardens *(left)* mix formality with more relaxed natural settings and boast a remarkable topiary sundial and stellar views.

The golden stone villages of the Cotswolds

The undulating green hills of the Cotswolds are a tourist honeypot. The area is, in many ways, a relic of times past, with meandering streams, rustic thatched cottages, wonderful churches, grand stately homes and graceful villages seemingly forgotten by time. This is picture-postcard Britain, but you'll need to take to the hills on foot if you'd like to lose your fellow visitors.

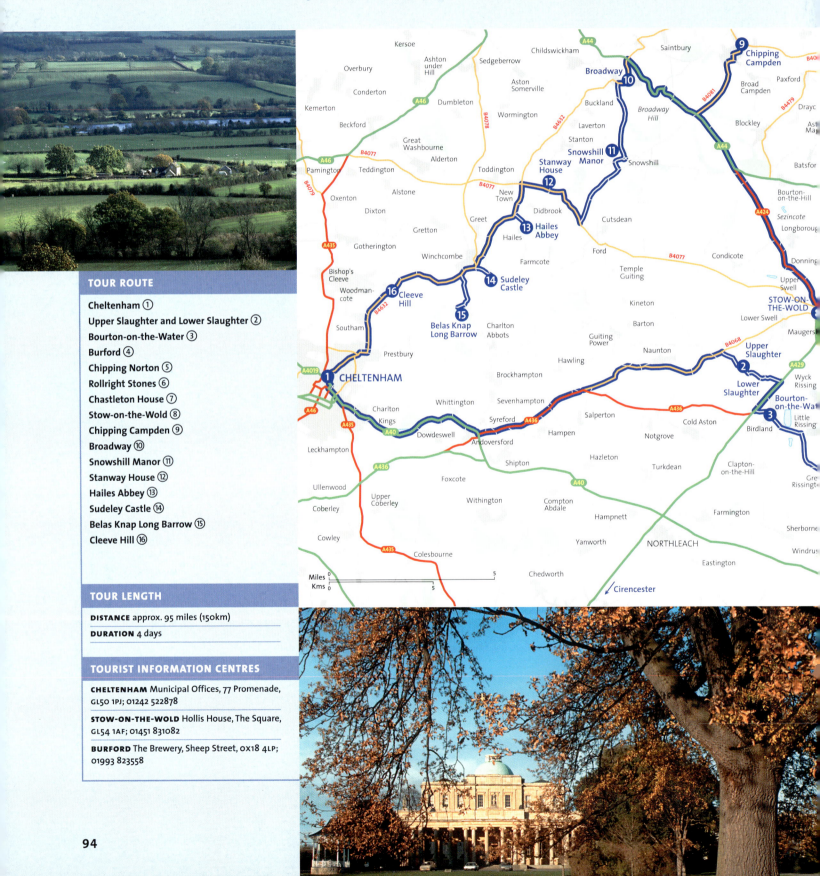

TOUR ROUTE

Cheltenham ①

Upper Slaughter and Lower Slaughter ②

Bourton-on-the-Water ③

Burford ④

Chipping Norton ⑤

Rollright Stones ⑥

Chastleton House ⑦

Stow-on-the-Wold ⑧

Chipping Campden ⑨

Broadway ⑩

Snowshill Manor ⑪

Stanway House ⑫

Hailes Abbey ⑬

Sudeley Castle ⑭

Belas Knap Long Barrow ⑮

Cleeve Hill ⑯

TOUR LENGTH

DISTANCE approx. 95 miles (150km)

DURATION 4 days

TOURIST INFORMATION CENTRES

CHELTENHAM Municipal Offices, 77 Promenade, GL50 1PJ; 01242 522878

STOW-ON-THE-WOLD Hollis House, The Square, GL54 1AF; 01451 831082

BURFORD The Brewery, Sheep Street, OX18 4LP; 01993 823558

Clockwise from far left:
Cotswolds scenery;
cottages in the south
Cotswolds; milestone,
Broadway; Pittville Pump
Room, Cheltenham

1 CHELTENHAM

Gloriously assured, impeccably polite and unfailingly graceful, the spa town of Cheltenham boasts a wealth of elegant architecture that helps maintain the city's air of exclusivity to this day. The healing waters here were discovered in 1716, and soon everyone wanted a piece of the pie – the rich and famous flocked to town, with the era's master builders in tow, to create the Regency masterpiece you see today.

The city is full of impressive buildings, elegant squares and terraces, and plenty of chichi boutiques. At its heart lies the majestic Promenade, a broad, sweeping street lined with handsome houses. Walking on from here you reach Montpellier, Cheltenham's most exclusive shopping district, where caryatids separate the boutiques on Montpellier Walk. Just off the Promenade is the **Cheltenham Art Gallery and Museum**. Its imaginative collection offers a wonderful insight into the social history of the city, and there's an excellent selection of Arts and Crafts furniture, ceramics and jewellery on display. Nearby is the **Holst Birthplace Museum**, where the composer was born in 1874. The museum houses displays on Holst's life and career but also gives you a glimpse of the interior of a restored Regency period house. From here, take a detour into the Regents Arcade to see the fascinating Kit Williams **Wishing Fish Clock**, with its balls, bubbles and animated mice, before heading slightly out of town to the **Pittville Pump Room,** Cheltenham's finest Regency building. Built between 1825 and 1830, it was intended as a spa and social centre for a development by politician Joseph Pitt that never quite took off. You can still taste the alkaline waters here, but the building and its grand ballroom are more often used for exhibitions and concerts. Cheltenham is also justly famous for horse racing, and in March each year it hosts the National Hunt Festival.

From Cheltenham, drive east on the A40, turning onto the A436 and then bearing left onto the B4068. Follow the signs from here to **Upper Slaughter.** **Lower Slaughter** *is just to the south east.*

→ • • • • • • • • • • • 2

Follow the signs from Lower Slaughter into **Bourton-on-the-Water**.

 Drive south east on minor roads through Great Rissington and Great Barrington onto the A424 to **Burford**.

 Follow the A361 north from Burford to reach **Chipping Norton**.

Head north on the B4026 and take the first minor road to the left for the **Rollright Stones**.

2 UPPER SLAUGHTER AND LOWER SLAUGHTER

The tiny villages of Upper and Lower Slaughter actually take their apparently rather ghoulish name from the Old English word for slough, and today the meandering River Windrush is one of their most photogenic features. Flanked by a Victorian flour mill and gorgeous cottages, it helps to make these two tiny villages some of the most picturesque in Britain. Stunning old manor houses survive in each village, and a walking trail leads through both of them down to Bourton and offers unique views of this idyllic part of the Cotswolds.

3 BOURTON-ON-THE-WATER

The gorgeous village of Bourton focuses on the meandering River Windrush, which flows quietly under a series of low bridges, right through the centre of the village. It is lined with mellow Cotswold buildings of honey-coloured stone with steeply pitched roofs, mullioned windows and immaculately kept gardens. However, Burton is one of the most visited spots in the Cotswolds, and it can be overrun in summer. Numerous other attractions, such as a **model village** and railway, the **Cotswold Motoring Museum** and the **Birdland Park and Gardens**, which showcases rare and exotic birds, draw even more visitors, so it's best to arrive at dawn or dusk if you want to see the village at its quietest.

4 BURFORD

Achingly picturesque but frustratingly besieged by visitors in summer, Burford is a stunning little town that slips down a steep hill to a medieval bridge over the River Windrush. The high street is lined with wonderful old rickety-roofed buildings that now house shops and cafes selling antiques, art, crafts and cream teas. The original market hall, the **Tolsey**, is home to a modest museum of local history, and further down the hill the striking **parish church** dates from Norman times with some 15th-century alterations. Inside, it is a warren of passageways and chambers and a secluded oasis from the hustle and bustle of the main drag.

5 CHIPPING NORTON

The bustling market town of Chipping Norton made its fortune from the medieval wool trade, and most of the sturdy stone houses and half-timbered inns that line the market square today were financed with the wealth it brought. Leading off the square, Church Street is flanked by a set of beautiful almshouses that lead down to one of the finest wool churches in the country: **St Mary's Parish Church** dates from the 15th century and has a wonderful Perpendicular nave and some well-preserved tombs. Just outside the town, the imposing 18th-century **Bliss Tweed Mill** with its giant chimney stack kick-started the town's textile industry. It now contains luxury apartments.

Clockwise from above left:
the River Windrush at
Bourton-on-the-Water;
Chastleton House;
Lower Slaughter

THE COTSWOLD UPLANDS

The rambling limestone uplands of the Cotswolds are the source of the mellow, honey-coloured stone that gives the region's towns and villages their distinctive character. However, the unique breed of sheep that still graze on the hilly slopes are equally responsible for the area's beauty. By medieval times the sheep had evolved into a strong, sturdy breed strengthened by the nutrient-rich grasses on the limestone pastures and adorned with a thick fleece to protect them from the wind. The quality of their fleece soon created a thriving wool trade, and local merchants grew rich on their profits and built the grand houses and fine churches that litter the region today.

6 ROLLRIGHT STONES

The twisted forms of the weathered stones at Rollright are an atmospheric sight, and although they make up one of the best-known stone circles in the country, you can often be their only visitor. The standing stones here date from about 2500BC and are arranged in two main groups: the King's Men, a stone circle, and the Whispering Men, a burial chamber. Nearby is a solitary standing stone, the King Stone, supposedly a petrified monarch trapped by the curse of an evil witch.

7 CHASTLETON HOUSE

Gloriously unkempt and just oozing character, 17th-century Chastleton was the home of the Jones family for 400 years. Although now under the care of the National Trust, the house has retained a wonderfully lived-in air, with walking sticks and Wellington boots lying around, the woodwork and pewter left unpolished, and bric-a-brac piled up on shelves. It is one of the most magnificent and complete Jacobean houses in Britain and is stuffed with elaborate plasterwork and panelling, fine tapestries and glassware, portraits and personal belongings. The gardens follow a typical Elizabethan and Jacobean layout with a topiary garden at their heart, whose claim to fame is being the place where the rules of croquet were first thrashed out.

Head south west on minor roads to join the A44 west and follow the signs left for **Chastleton House**.

Drive south east from Chastleton on minor roads to join the A436 west into **Stow-on-the-Wold**.

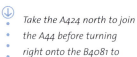

Take the A424 north to join the A44 before turning right onto the B4081 to **Chipping Campden**.

⑨

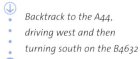

Backtrack to the A44, driving west and then turning south on the B4632 ⑩ *to reach* **Broadway**.

Take the minor road uphill from the village green in Broadway to **Snowshill Manor**.

  ⑪

8 STOW-ON-THE-WOLD

The gorgeous hilltop market town of Stow-on-the-Wold is a favourite with passing tourists drawn here by its beautiful buildings and the antique shops and galleries that line the streets surrounding the lovely market square. A network of narrow lanes around the square were used to funnel sheep into the market, and the medieval cross at its centre reminded traders to be fair in their transactions. In 1646, the town was the site of the last battle of Charles I's army in the Civil War, and most of the buildings here date from that time.

9 CHIPPING CAMPDEN

Unassuming Chipping Campden is a delightful place that refuses to bow to commercialism and manages to retain a real sense of how Cotswold wool towns might have looked in their heyday. The long, gently curving high street is flanked with a host of listed buildings dating from between the 14th and 17th centuries, while on the lanes behind you'll find gorgeous thatched cottages and ancient almshouses. The highlight, though, is the town's magnificent Perpendicular church, built at the height of the wool trade in the 15th century.

10 BROADWAY

Known as the 'Jewel of the Cotswolds', Broadway is one of the prettiest villages in the area and was an inspiration to writers and artists such as Henry James, J M Barrie and William Morris. The wide main drag is lined with red chestnut trees and honey-coloured buildings from medieval, Tudor and Georgian times. Most of these now house antiques shops, art galleries and chichi boutiques, but one of the best experiences in the area is to follow the footpath from town for a bracing walk up Broadway Hill. En route you'll pass the medieval **Church of St Eadburgha** before ascending to **Broadway Tower,** a Gothic folly that offers views over 13 counties. The tower was a country retreat used by William Morris, and an exhibition inside details his connections with the area.

Clockwise from far left:
Broadway Tower; view of
street, Chipping Campden;
church detail, Stanway;
interior, Stanway House

THE ARTS AND CRAFTS MOVEMENT

The Arts and Crafts movement rejected the opulent, mass-produced designs of the Victorian era and instead favoured simple, individual style and quality craftsmanship. William Morris, the 19th-century socialist, poet and craftsman who spearheaded the movement, had his country home at Kelmscott in the south Cotswolds, and many other designers, artists and craftsmen followed suit and settled in the area. Between them they left behind a rich legacy of Arts and Crafts works, from the much-loved work of C R Ashbee and his followers in Chipping Campden to the treasures of the south Cotswolds: Owlpen Manor *(see p105)*, Rodmarton Manor and Selsey Church. The Cheltenham Art Gallery and Museum *(see p95)* also has a wonderful collection of Arts and Crafts furniture, jewellery, books and pottery.

11 SNOWSHILL MANOR

Stuffed with the weird and wonderful collection of the famously eccentric Charles Paget Wade, Snowshill Manor is a remarkable place with a vast treasure trove of objects on display. Wade collected artefacts from around the world and eventually had to move out of the cluttered house as his collection took over all available space. Period costumes, children's prams, wooden toys, musical instruments and Japanese armour adorn the rooms of this traditional Cotswold house, while outside the Arts and Crafts-style garden is divided into 'rooms' by a series of terraces and ponds.

12 STANWAY HOUSE

The tiny village of **Stanway** is home to a wonderful Jacobean manor house nestled at the foot of the hills and surrounded by an elaborate gatehouse, church and tithe barn. Stanway House remains largely untouched and is still full of its original furniture, but the grand 18th-century water gardens, which are slowly being restored, are the biggest draw. Thought to have been designed by Charles Bridgeman, one of the foremost gardeners of his time, the gardens boast the highest fountain in Britain, a formal canal, and an unusual pyramid folly that leads to a lengthy cascade.

Follow minor roads south
to join the B4077 west to
Stanway House.

Continue west on the
B4077, joining the B4632
south and following the
signs for Hailes Abbey.

 Return to the B4632 and continue south from Hailes to Winchcombe, then follow the signs for **Sudeley Castle**.

Backtrack to the B4632 and drive south, turning left after 1 mile for **Belas Knap Long Barrow**.

13 HAILES ABBEY

All that now remains of the once-celebrated pilgrimage site of Hailes Abbey are the cloister arches, standing proud against a backdrop of the Cotswold Hills. The abbey was founded in 1246, and thanks to its hoard of phials of Christ's blood (later revealed to be a mixture of honey and saffron) the Cistercian monastery grew to be one of England's most important. The abbey was destroyed during the Dissolution, however, and a small museum on the site now explains its history. Nearby is a church dating from 1300 that contains some beautiful wall paintings.

14 SUDELEY CASTLE

Set against a backdrop of the Cotswold Hills and surrounded by stunning gardens, 15th-century Sudeley Castle was a favourite retreat of Tudor and Stuart monarchs. The castle was once home to Katherine Parr, Henry VIII's sixth wife, and her tomb lies in the gorgeous chapel in the gardens. Inside the fortified manor house, exhibitions of Victoriana and great master paintings adorn the rooms, but it is the stunning Queen's Garden that really draws the crowds. Sculpted yews, glorious roses and evocative ruins set the scene, while further up the hill the remains of a Roman villa, now largely overgrown, can be explored.

Clockwise from far left:
the ruin of Hailes Abbey;
Sudeley Castle; a fountain in
the gardens, Sudeley Castle

15 BELAS KNAP LONG BARROW

It's a two-and-a-half-mile hike from Winchcombe to the Neolithic long barrow at Belas Knap, one of the best preserved burial chambers in England. The barrow dates from about 3000BC and contains four burial chambers that once held up to 40 people. Although you cannot go inside the barrow, the views from here of the surrounding countryside and down over Sudeley Castle are spectacular, and ample reward for your walk.

Return again to the B4632 and drive south to reach Cleeve Hill. 16

16 CLEEVE HILL

Some of the best walking and the most spectacular views in the Cotswolds can be enjoyed from Cleeve Common, the highest point (330m; 1,085ft) in the escarpment. Here the ridge rises steeply from the valley floor and offers dramatic vistas down over Winchcombe, and as far as Gloucester Cathedral, the Malvern Hills and the Black Mountains in Wales.

Continue on the same road for 4 miles to return to Cheltenham.
1

WITH MORE TIME

Cirencester *(left)*, to the south west of the tour, was once a major Roman town known as Corinium, and one of its biggest attractions is the Corinium Museum, which is full of fascinating finds. There is also an impressive Roman amphitheatre just to the west. Today, the town is dominated by its 15th-century wool church – an impressive building with a collection of intricately decorated chapels. Cirencester is known for its crafts, too: several craftsmen's workshops are open to the public at the Brewery Arts Centre, and there are craft markets in the nearby Corn Hall on Saturdays.

Rustic charm in the Severn Valley

The green, rolling hills of this part of Gloucestershire are steeped in history and strewn liberally with picturesque villages, country piles, crumbling castles and ancient forests. This is rural England at its very finest: virtually untouched by tourism and oozing quiet country charm. There is architectural grandeur and heritage aplenty, but for most visitors this part of the world is less about the cultural legacy and more about the refreshingly simple stone villages of the south Cotswolds, the lush greenery of the Wye Valley and the mystery of the Forest of Dean.

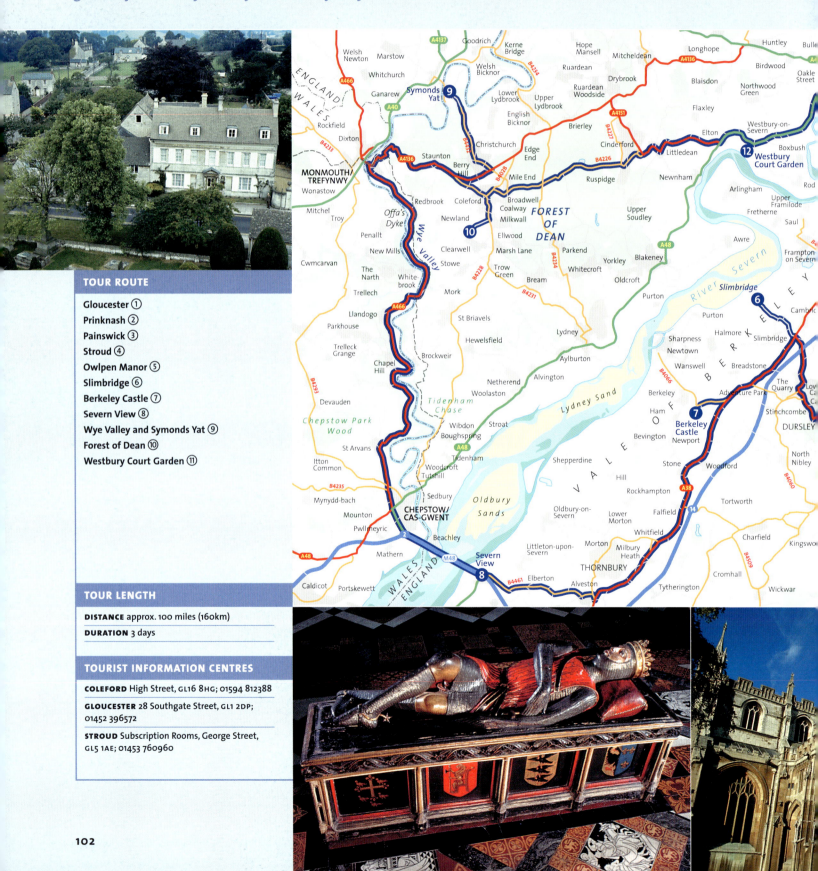

TOUR ROUTE

Gloucester ①
Prinknash ②
Painswick ③
Stroud ④
Owlpen Manor ⑤
Slimbridge ⑥
Berkeley Castle ⑦
Severn View ⑧
Wye Valley and Symonds Yat ⑨
Forest of Dean ⑩
Westbury Court Garden ⑪

TOUR LENGTH

DISTANCE approx. 100 miles (160km)

DURATION 3 days

TOURIST INFORMATION CENTRES

COLEFORD High Street, GL16 8HG; 01594 812388

GLOUCESTER 28 Southgate Street, GL1 2DP; 01452 396572

STROUD Subscription Rooms, George Street, GL5 1AE; 01453 760960

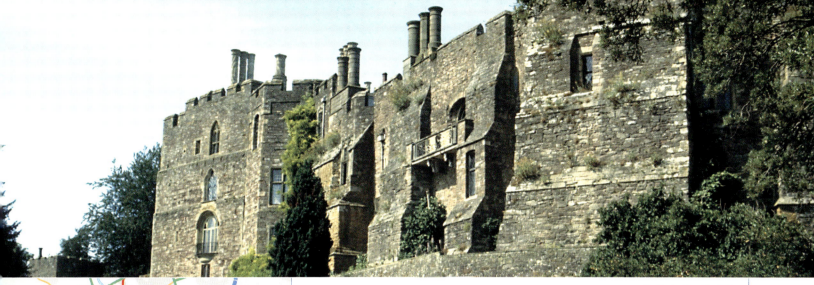

1 GLOUCESTER

1
GLOUCESTER

Although Gloucester stands on the site of an ancient settlement, little remains of the Roman and Saxon towns that once thrived here. Today, the city is a down-to-earth kind of place dominated by its majestic Gothic **cathedral**. Founded by Benedictine monks in 1069, the original Norman church hosted the coronation of nine-year-old Henry III in 1216 and the burial of unpopular Edward II in 1327, after he was murdered at Berkeley Castle *(see p105)*. The church soon became a place of pilgrimage, raising enough funds to finance its transformation into the incredible structure you see today. Although the nave remains a sturdy Norman construct, the glorious Great Cloister with its wonderful fan vaulting dates from the 14th-century. Other additions include a whispering gallery, a 15th-century Lady's Chapel and a tower with fantastic views over the city. The 25m-tall great east window (80ft) is England's largest medieval window, and in the Tribune Gallery there's an exhibition on the making of the window and the history of the cathedral.

Nearby on Ladybellgate Street you'll find **Blackfriars**, the most complete medieval Dominican priory in the country. Further south is the **Gloucester Docks**, an area of Victorian warehouses around the canal basins, now buzzing with restaurants, bars, shops and an antiques centre. For a fascinating insight into 18th- and 19th-century life and the huge role the canals played in it, visit the **National Waterways Museum** before heading back into town to see the **House of the Tailor of Gloucester**, the inspiration for one of Beatrix Potter's stories. The house is now a homage to the author and her delightful little books.

Clockwise from far left: view of Painswick from the church tower; Berkeley Castle; the Gloucester Docks; Gloucester Cathedral; tomb, Gloucester Cathedral

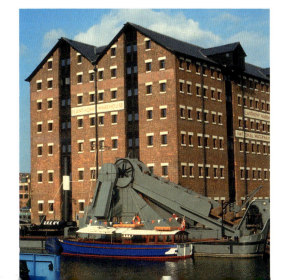

*Leave Gloucester on the B4073 south east to Upton St Leonards, then follow the minor road to **Prinknash**.*

2 PRINKNASH

The Benedictine **abbey** at Prinknash was once famous for its pottery, but this has not been produced here since the late 1990s, and Prinknash is now better known as the oldest major incense blender in Europe. For visitors, however, the main attraction is the Orpheus Pavement, a life-size reproduction of the 205-sq-m (2,200-sq-ft) Roman mosaic now buried to prevent deterioration at nearby Woodchester. The original pavement, part of a Roman villa, dates from AD325 and has been uncovered only seven times since its discovery. Surrounding the abbey there's a 160-ha (400-acre) bird and deer park with glorious views across the Severn Vale.

*Drive south for
3 miles on the A46
to Painswick.*

3 PAINSWICK

The old wool town of Painswick is a warren of medieval streets set on a steep, wooded hill and has come to be known as the 'Queen of the Cotswolds'. The town's focal point is **St Mary's Church**, famous for its 18th-century tabletop tombs and 99 yew trees, but the narrow streets that surround it are well worth seeking out for their old merchant houses and charming cottages. Just outside the town is the ostentatious **Painswick Rococo Garden** designed by Benjamin Hyett in the 18th century. The restored gardens are laid out following strict geometric patterns, and also feature a maze and a series of beautiful architectural follies.

*Continue on the A46
south to reach **Stroud**.*

SEVERN BORE

The Severn bore is one of Britain's most impressive natural phenomena, and occurs when tide water sweeps up the Severn channel, rising as the channel narrows and causing the formation of a series of fast-moving waves. The highest tides, and consequently the largest bores, occur a few days after new and full moons. The most spectacular bores can be seen around the spring and autumn equinoxes, when surfers, body-boarders and canoeists line up and attempt to catch the waves. The largest bore ever recorded reached a height of over 2.75m (9ft). For the best views look for the bore between Awre, where the estuary begins to narrow, and Gloucester.

*Clockwise from below:
view of Painswick from
the hill above the town;
Owlpen; bust of Sir Peter
Scott, Slimbridge*

4 STROUD

The five wooded valleys surrounding Stroud (pronounced 'Strowd') give it a gorgeous location, and one littered with the remnants of its heyday as the centre of the local textile industry. At the height of the wool trade there were 150 woollen mills here and the town prospered on the profits of the industry. Many of the old mills are still visible, and you can find out more about them at the fascinating **Museum in the Park**, an innovative place that tells the story of the town and the area. Stroud has also become something of a centre for alternative living, with a progressive council, plenty of New Agers and a host of venues selling organic foods and fair trade goods.

5 OWLPEN MANOR

Nestled in the lee of the Cotswold hills, Owlpen Manor is a romantic Tudor house surrounded by formal terraced gardens and medieval buildings. In 1926, Arts and Crafts architect Norman Jewson rescued and restored the manor after it had been left uninhabited for over 100 years, and a strong Arts and Crafts influence is visible in the furniture and fittings. One of the manor's highlights is the Tudor Great Hall, with its magnificent painted wall hangings. The room is supposedly haunted by Queen Margaret of Anjou, wife of Henry VI, who visited Owlpen in 1471, shortly before the Battle of Tewkesbury led to the loss of her freedom and fortune. Also worth seeking out are the Jacobean wing and the charming Georgian Little Parlour.

6 SLIMBRIDGE

Britain's largest wildlife sanctuary, the Slimbridge nature reserve was founded in 1946 by Sir Peter Scott, a conservationist and founder of the Wildfowl and Wetlands Trust. The 49ha (120 acres) of protected wetlands on the banks of the Severn Estuary attract an enormous collection of birds and are an important wintering area for migrating waterbirds such as the Bewick's Swan. Bird-watching hides dotted around the reserve allow visitors to see the swans, geese and ducks at close range, while the visitor centre has details of the conservation programmes at work.

7 BERKELEY CASTLE

Site of the grisly murder of Edward II and still owned by the Berkeley family, the 12th-century Berkeley Castle is a one-time Norman fortress turned into a family home. It was in 1327 that Queen Isabella and her lover impaled poor Edward on a red-hot poker and left him for dead in one of the cells. Almost 700 years later, however, the castle is an oasis of peace and calm, ringed by terraced gardens and sweeping lawns, and it houses a formidable collection of paintings by English and Dutch masters, plus impressive furniture and tapestries. Nearby is the **Jenner Museum**, former home of Dr Edward Jenner, and the place where he created the first smallpox vaccine in 1796.

Drive south west on the B4066 towards Uley and follow the signs for **Owlpen Manor**. 5

Continue west on the B4066, then take the A4135 north west to the junction with the A38 and follow the signs for **Slimbridge**. 6

Return to the A38 and drive south before turning right onto the B4066 to **Berkeley Castle**. 7

Back track to the A38 and drive south to Alveston, where you join the B4461 west to **Severn View**. 8

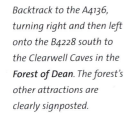

*Join the M48 at junction 1 and cross the Severn Bridge to Chepstow. Drive north on the A466, which follows the **Wye Valley** along the border with Wales. Pick up the A4136 at Monmouth, then turn left onto the*

9 *B4432 to **Symonds Yat**.*

*Backtrack to the A4136, turning right and then left onto the B4228 south to the Clearwell Caves in the **Forest of Dean**. The forest's other attractions are clearly signposted.*

→ • • • • • • • • • • • **10**

8 SEVERN VIEW

It's worth making a quick stop at the Severn View service area for the spectacular views over the river and its two imposing bridges. The first Severn Bridge opened in 1966, and since then it has carried more than 300 million vehicles. However, problems with congestion, instability in high winds and accidents meant that a second bridge was opened in 1996.

9 WYE VALLEY AND SYMONDS YAT

Heading north from Chepstow you'll drive along the scenic Wye Valley, an Area of Outstanding Natural Beauty and a glorious but brief diversion into Wales. The Wye is one of Britain's least spoilt rivers, and here the wooded slopes of the valley afford wonderful views at every turn. The biggest viewpoint on this stretch of the river is Symonds Yat Rock, a wooded limestone outcrop high above the valley, which is famous for its spectacular views of the surrounding countryside. Peregrine falcons nest nearby and can be seen flying around the rock during the summer months, while down below at Symonds Yat East, a rope ferry transports visitors across the river. At Symonds Yat West there is a visitor centre and maze.

OFFA'S DYKE

Skirting along the ancient border between England and Wales, Offa's Dyke is a monumental earthwork that runs 177 miles from Prestatyn to Chepstow. Today a national trail follows the route of the 8th-century earthworks and it can be easily accessed from Brockweir and Redbrook in the Forest of Dean. This seven-mile section makes an excellent day hike and offers beautiful views over the surrounding countryside.

10 FOREST OF DEAN

The ancient royal hunting grounds in the Forest of Dean are a magical place, dripping with mystery and supposedly the inspiration for the setting of J R R Tolkien's *Lord of the Rings*. The 42 sq miles of forest were once used for iron and coal mining, but an excellent network of tracks and many impressive views now make them ideal for walking and cycling. One of the forest's best-known attractions, the **Clearwell Caves and Ancient Iron Mines** are a series of atmospheric natural caves enlarged by mining and worth a tour to see their unusual rock formations and underground pools. Nearby in the pretty village of Newland you'll find the 13th-century All Saints Church, known locally as the '**Cathedral of the Forest**' thanks to its grand proportions. Look out for the 'miner's boss' inside, which dipicts a forest miner with a candle in his mouth, a pick axe and a hod. **Puzzle Wood** is a mysterious set of trails through an overgrown pre-Roman open cast iron mine. If you prefer more artistic attractions, the **Sculpture Trail**, starting at the Beechenhurst Lodge, runs through majestic oaks and pines and is lined with specially commissioned sculptures. You can also take llama tours of the forest from here. In Upper Soudley, stop off at the **Dean Heritage Centre**, which does an excellent job of explaining the history of the forest.

11 WESTBURY COURT GARDEN

The rare Dutch water garden at Westbury Court was originally laid out between 1696 and 1705 and is the only one of its kind in Britain to have been fully restored. The gardens are also home to many 16th and 17th-century trees and shrubs as well as rare varieties of apple, pear and plum. The highlight of the gardens, however, is the yew-lined canal headed by a Dutch-style pavilion. Also look out for the secret walled garden and the holm oak, supposedly the oldest in the country.

Clockwise from above:
the walled garden at
Westbury Court Garden;
joggers on the Sculpture
Trail, Forest of Dean;
'cathedral' sculpture, Forest
of Dean; Symonds Yat

Take the B4226 east through
the forest, continuing
onto the A4151 to reach
Westbury Court Garden. **11**

Take the A48 from
Westbury Court Garden
*back into **Gloucester**.*
 **1**

WITH MORE TIME

The 240ha (600 acres) of temperate forest gardens at **Westonbirt Arboretum** *(left)* were founded in 1829 by landowner Robert Holford, and since then, the collection of trees and shrubs has grown into a magnificent array of exotic species, leafy glades and glorious blooms. With 17 miles of trails crisscrossing the site, it is a beautiful place for walking at any time of year, but is best-known for its incredible displays of colour in springtime, when the bluebells, azaleas, rhododendrons, camellias and magnolias come out in force, and in autumn, when the maples turn fiery red.

Warwickshire, Worcestershire, Herefordshire and Shropshire

Around Stratford-upon-Avon: in the footsteps of the Bard

Heritage-rich Warwickshire is home to some of the most popular tourist destinations in England, including both Shakespeare's home and the mighty Warwick Castle. But there is so much more to discover than these headline acts. This region has been a longtime favourite haunt of royalty and the wealthy, who have left behind them many fine merchant houses, impressive stately homes and glorious hidden villages.

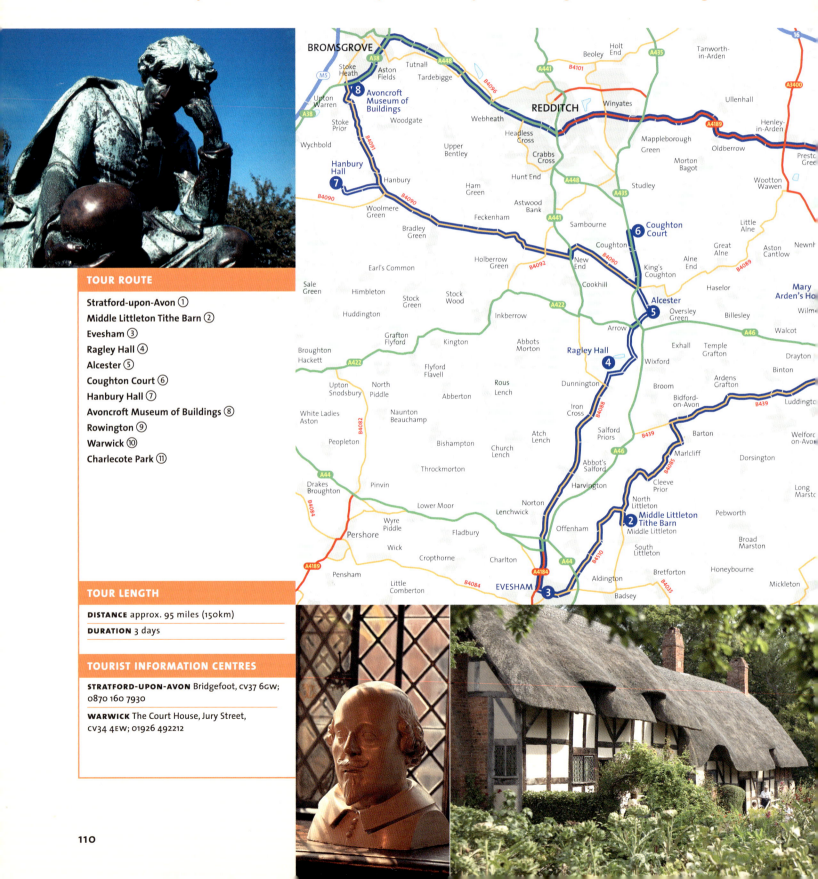

TOUR ROUTE

Stratford-upon-Avon ①
Middle Littleton Tithe Barn ②
Evesham ③
Ragley Hall ④
Alcester ⑤
Coughton Court ⑥
Hanbury Hall ⑦
Avoncroft Museum of Buildings ⑧
Rowington ⑨
Warwick ⑩
Charlecote Park ⑪

TOUR LENGTH

DISTANCE approx. 95 miles (150km)
DURATION 3 days

TOURIST INFORMATION CENTRES

STRATFORD-UPON-AVON Bridgefoot, cv37 6gw; 0870 160 7930

WARWICK The Court House, Jury Street, cv34 4ew; 01926 492212

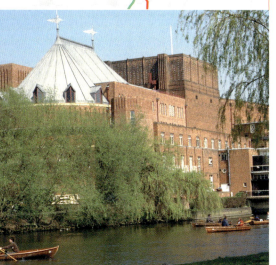

1 STRATFORD-UPON-AVON

World famous as Shakespeare's birthplace, Stratford-upon-Avon is a well-preserved riverside market town that luckily has plenty of historic houses to entertain the busloads of tourists. The town's top attraction is, naturally, the museum at **Shakespeare's Birthplace**, housed in a modern building attached to the half-timbered house where the great man was born. The museum details Shakespeare's life and works, while the house itself is decked out in typical 16th-century style. Close by is **New Place**, where Shakespeare had his final home. Only the foundations of the original house are visible, but beside them is **Nash's House**, which was home to his granddaughter Elizabeth and is now full of 17th-century furniture and tapestries, plus an exhibition on the town's history. **Hall's Croft**, the beautiful 17th-century townhouse that was once home to the Bard's daughter Susanna, contains the fascinating collections of her husband Dr John Hall, which document medical practice in Elizabethan times. A further pilgrimage site on the Shakespeare trail is the **Holy Trinity Church**, a lovely 13th-century riverside church where Shakespeare and his wife are buried. You can see some of his plays performed at the **Royal Shakespeare Theatre** or **The Swan**, a modern theatre cast in the mould of an Elizabethan playhouse. Both are run by the Royal Shakespeare Company, one of the world's best-known classical theatre groups, and you can also take backstage tours for a behind-the-scenes look at the RSC, its costumes and its props. Just outside town is **Anne Hathaway's Cottage**, a timeless thatched cottage and garden that was the childhood home of Shakespeare's wife.

Among Stratford's non-literary attractions is **Harvard House**, the home of the mother of John Harvard, who gave his name to the prestigious US university. The ornate half-timbered Elizabethan townhouse is now home to the Museum of British Pewter. Also worth a look is the **Teddy Bear Museum** with its slightly eerie collection of stuffed bears, and the **Stratford Butterfly Farm**, one of the largest in Europe, with its collection of rare butterflies, insects and spiders. Despite the many worthy museums and houses in this part of the world, one of the most pleasant places to while away a sunny afternoon in Stratford is in a rowing boat on the River Avon.

Clockwise from far left: statue, Stratford-upon-Avon; Warwick Castle; the River Avon and the Royal Shakespeare Theatre, Stratford; Anne Hathaway's Cottage; bust of Shakespeare, Shakespeare's Birthplace Museum

Head west from Stratford on the B439, turn left in Bidford-on-Avon onto the B4085, and follow the signs to Middle Littleton Tithe Barn.

Clockwise from above:
half-timbered building,
Evesham; Coughton Court

⊕ Take the B4510 south
   from Middle Littleton
③ to reach **Evesham**.

Head north on the A4184
and then the B4088 to
Dunnington and follow
the signs for **Ragley Hall**.

→ • • • • • • • • • • • • ④

WILLIAM SHAKESPEARE

Lauded as one of the finest writers of all time, William Shakespeare (1564–1616, *below*) has become a household name across the globe, his works translated into all major languages and his popularity undiminished even hundreds of years after his death. However, controversy still reigns over who Shakespeare really was. Little documentary evidence exists other than his birth, death and marriage certificates, and many scholars claim that a humble country boy from Stratford would never have had the knowledge to write so convincingly about foreign countries and the goings-on in royal circles. Sir Francis Bacon, Christopher Marlowe and Edward de Vere have all been mooted as possible authors of the works, yet no one can find decisive evidence for any claim. Regardless of who the author really was, the plays and poems attributed to Shakespeare are some of the greatest ever to be written in the English language, showing an extraordinary understanding of human nature and the ways of the world.

2 MIDDLE LITTLETON TITHE BARN

One of the largest and finest tithe barns in the country, this beautifully constructed 13th-century building at Middle Littleton combines wonderful interior timber framing, gabled double doors and slender ventilation shafts. The enormous barn was used as a storage space for tithes collected across the parish as a tax for the church. It is now of interest for its architectural detail.

3 EVESHAM

The River Avon sweeps through the historic market town of Evesham, once home to the third largest abbey in England. A monastery was founded here in the 8th century, after the Virgin Mary appeared to a swineherd, and by the time the abbey was dissolved in 1540 it had grown into a powerful base. Today, the site is a tranquil park and all that remains of its former glory are the twin churches of All Saints and St Lawrence and a lovely 16th-century bell tower. For some history on the abbey, visit the gorgeous **Almonry Museum and Heritage Centre**, a 14th-century building with a fine museum detailing the abbey's past as well as the defeat of Simon de Montfort in the battle of Evesham in 1265. Elsewhere in the town there are some fine half-timbered 15th-century houses.

4 RAGLEY HALL

This grand neo-Palladian mansion was designed by Robert Hooke in 1680 and is the family home of the marquess and marchioness of Hertford. James Wyatt was employed to remodel the Red Saloon and add a portico in 1780, while the vast Great Hall showcases the extravagant Baroque plasterwork of James Gibbs. Further Baroque decoration can be seen in the elaborate ceilings and chimneypieces throughout the house. There is also a fine collection of 18th-century paintings and antiques on display. On the South Staircase you can see the powerful mural *The Temptation* by Graham Rust, while outside, formal gardens and rolling parkland surround the house.

5 ALCESTER

Historic Alcester is set on the River Arrow and retains much of its medieval network of streets, many of them lined with half-timbered Tudor houses. At the centre of town is the pretty Church of St Nicholas with its 14th-century tower, and nearby is the sturdy early-17th-century Town Hall. Alcester began life as a Roman settlement and the local **Heritage Centre** explains the town's history and its well-documented Roman past.

6 COUGHTON COURT

The stunning turreted Tudor mansion at Coughton Court has been home to the staunchly Catholic Throckmarton family since 1409. Their religious views, and support of the Gunpowder Plot in 1605, played an important part in the history of the house. It suffered fire damage when the Parliamentarians occupied the building during the English Civil War, and had its east wing destroyed by a Protestant mob in 1688. There is also a series of priest holes used for hiding Catholic clergy. A fascinating exhibition tells you the history of the Gunpowder Plot and the family's close associations with its leaders. The half-timbered courtyard boasts a magnificent central gatehouse dating from 1530, while the grounds have been restored in keeping with the character of the house. Here you can explore a wonderful walled garden, a labyrinth, a bog garden and some delightful riverside walks.

*Turn left as you leave Ragley and drive through the village of Arrow into **Alcester**.* **5**

*Drive north to pick up the A435 to **Coughton Court**.* **6**

*Backtrack to Alcester and take the B4090 west to Hanbury, from where you can take minor roads to reach **Hanbury Hall**.*

↓

Backtrack to Hanbury and drive north on the B4091, following the signs for the Avoncroft Museum of Buildings.

⑧

7 HANBURY HALL

William and Mary-style Hanbury Hall was completed in 1701 and is most famous for its beautifully executed wall and ceiling paintings – the work of Sir James Thornhill. In the Long Gallery is an exhibition about the history of the house, plus the Watney collection of fine porcelain and paintings, while outside are extensive parklands complete with a working mushroom house, an ice house, an orangery and restored 18th-century formal gardens. Nearby, in the village of Hanbury, is the **Jinny Ring Craft Centre**, where 12 craft studios, a gallery and a restaurant offer distractions of a different kind.

8 AVONCROFT MUSEUM OF BUILDINGS

Take the A38 then the A448 east to Redditch. From there, take the A4189 east to Preston Green, then turn left and go through Preston Bagot to Lowsonford and over the M40 to Rowington.

→ ⑨

The open-air museum at Avoncroft is home to a collection of restored buildings spanning seven centuries. A timber-framed house offers a glimpse of medieval life, and there's also a working windmill, a Victorian church and jail, and a 19th-century craftsmen's workshop. In addition, the museum is home to the national collection of telephone kiosks, which gives pride of place to Dr Who's *Tardis*.

9 ROWINGTON

The charming village of Rowington is presided over by St Laurence's Church, perched on top of a hill at the heart of the village. The half-timbered **Shakespeare Hall** was home to a branch of the Bard's family at one time, and local lore suggests that he wrote *As You Like It* here. The picturesque village is surrounded by rolling countryside and offers access to the scenic Grand Union Canal for some great leisurely walks.

10 WARWICK

Warwick is a wonderfully welcoming town dominated by its **castle**, but also home to many other historic buildings and museums. The massive medieval castle is one of Britain's most popular attractions, wonderfully preserved and brought to life by Madame Tussaud's waxworks and plenty of period furniture. The original Norman castle was fortified and extended in the 14th century, and elaborately reworked again in the 19th century. You can climb the towers and walk the ramparts, but most visitors head for the two waxwork displays – the 'Royal Weekend Party', which re-creates a party that took place here in 1898, and the 'Kingmaker Experience', which follows the Earl of Warwick's preparations for battle in 1471. The Great Hall, state rooms, bedrooms and dungeons can also be visited and are packed with antiques, portraits and armory.

Just outside the castle walls on the High Street is a cluster of crooked 14th-century half-timbered buildings known as the **Lord Leycester Hospital**. This served as an almshouse during the 16th century, and is worth a visit today for its history and stunning interiors – the guildhall and chapel are particular highlights. On the Market Place is the **Market Hall Museum**, housed in the 17th-century Market Hall. There are displays on local natural history and geology as well as an exhibition on Warwick's Great Fire of 1694. The nearby **Collegiate Church of St Mary** was largely destroyed in the fire and rebuilt in a mishmash of architectural styles, but its chancel survived untouched and the 15th-century Beauchamp Chapel contains a series of beautiful tombs. Back towards the castle, on Jury Street, is the **Warwickshire Yeomanry Museum**, which houses a fine collection of uniforms and arms. Finally, **St John's House Museum** is a grand Jacobean mansion refurbished in Victorian style and filled with exhibits on everything from period costumes to local history.

Clockwise from far left:
Warwick Castle; Charlecote Park; the Great Hall, Warwick Castle

11 CHARLECOTE PARK

Family home of the Lucys for more than 700 years, Charlecote Park is a majestic Tudor house encircled by landscaped gardens and its own deer park. Thomas Lucy started work on the present house in 1551, and although it was later given an overhaul in early Victorian style, the great chimneys, octagonal corner turrets and cupolas remain decidedly 16th-century. Inside, however, Victorian exuberance is everywhere, from the elaborate plasterwork to the large collection of family portraits. The house has connections with Queen Elizabeth I, who stayed here for two nights in 1572, and with Shakespeare, who was supposedly once caught poaching in the grounds.

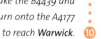
*Take the B4439 and turn onto the A4177 to reach **Warwick**.* ⑩

*Drive south on the A46, then the A429, and turn right onto the minor road to **Charlecote Park**.* ⑪

*Continue west on the B4088 and B4086 to return to **Stratford**.*

⬅ • • • • • • • • • • • • ①

WITH MORE TIME

A few miles from Stratford in the village of Wilmcote is the former home of Mary Arden, Shakespeare's mother. She inherited the house and land here on her father's death and, suddenly finding herself with a large dowry, soon found a husband in John Shakespeare. The Tudor farmhouse, known today as **Mary Arden's House** *(left)*, is now a museum of farm and family life in the 16th century. Next door, Palmer's House (once thought to be Mary Arden's house) can also be visited, and there's a well-preserved dovecote and cider press in the outbuildings, plus a rare breeds farm.

Warwickshire: from royal spa to classic cars

The north of Warwickshire has seen waves of glory over the centuries, and the vestiges of past wealth and royal connections are still in evidence today. But this region is not all about the distant past: more recently, the West Midlands motor industry has made it a real hotspot for classic car and motorbike enthusiasts. Nowhere is the county's unique combination of old and new more apparent than in the glorious twin cathedrals in Coventry.

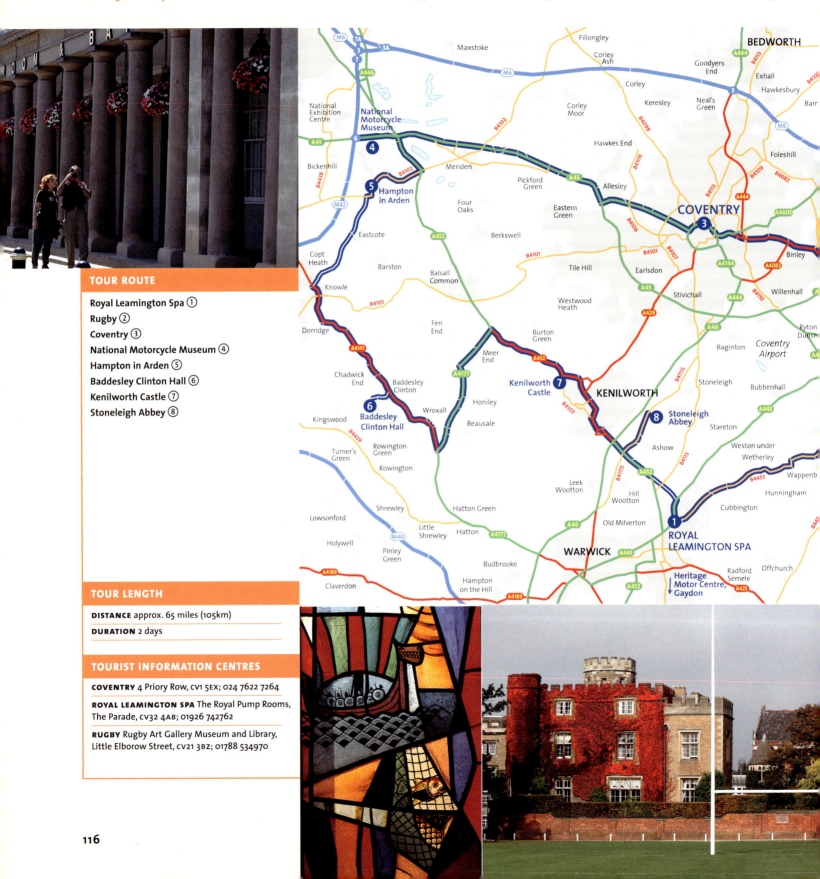

TOUR ROUTE

Royal Leamington Spa ①
Rugby ②
Coventry ③
National Motorcycle Museum ④
Hampton in Arden ⑤
Baddesley Clinton Hall ⑥
Kenilworth Castle ⑦
Stoneleigh Abbey ⑧

TOUR LENGTH

DISTANCE approx. 65 miles (105km)

DURATION 2 days

TOURIST INFORMATION CENTRES

COVENTRY 4 Priory Row, CV1 5EX; 024 7622 7264

ROYAL LEAMINGTON SPA The Royal Pump Rooms, The Parade, CV32 4AB; 01926 742762

RUGBY Rugby Art Gallery Museum and Library, Little Elborow Street, CV21 3BZ; 01788 534970

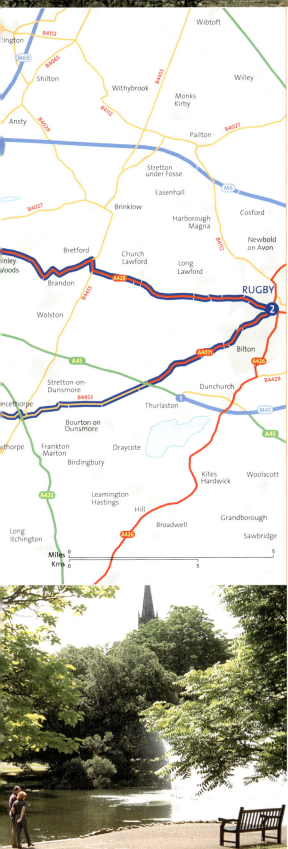

1 ROYAL LEAMINGTON SPA

Leamington Spa, once a small agricultural village, came into its own when the saline springs here were tapped in the early 19th century to provide an opportunity for visitors to 'take the cure'. Although the baths have long since closed, the genteel wide streets, fine Regency and Victorian architecture and wonderful parks and gardens financed by the crowds who flocked here make it worthy of a visit. In the centre of the town is a statue of Queen Victoria, who gave the town its 'royal' prefix. The elegant **Royal Pump Rooms** have recently been restored, and you can visit the Assembly Room and Turkish bath room. The building also houses a museum and art gallery with changing exhibitions. Just over the road are the prettily laid out **Jephson Gardens** – the highlight of a town renowned for its parks. The new lakeside pavilion here has a glasshouse featuring a wide variety of sub-tropical plants, and this is also a great place to enjoy a relaxing stroll along the River Leam.

Leave Leamington Spa on the B4453, heading north east, and then pick up the A4071 to reach Rugby. **2**

2 RUGBY

Rugby's best-known landmark is its school, founded in the 16th century and still one of the most prestigious in the country. It was the setting for Thomas Hughes's *Tom Brown's Schooldays*, but is much more famous as the place where William Webb Ellis supposedly picked up a ball and ran with it during a game of football in 1823, giving rise to the game of rugby football. The **Rugby School Museum** tells the tale in full detail and charts how the gentleman's game, and the school, developed over the years. You can also take a tour of the grand classrooms, atmospheric old library and beautiful chapel. Nearby, the **Webb Ellis Rugby Football Museum** has even more information on the sport, with a series of rooms stuffed with old photographs and memorabilia of every kind. Between the two museums is a statue of Webb Ellis himself. Also in the town is the **Rugby Art Gallery and Museum**, which has a wonderful collection of Roman artefacts as well as 20th-century British art.

Take the A428 west to Coventry. **3**

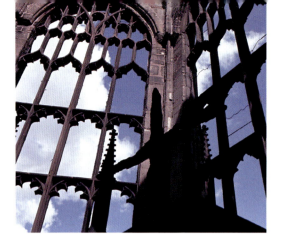

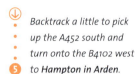

Drive west onto the A45 and continue to the M42 junction, from where you can follow the signposts to the **National Motorcycle Museum**. ④

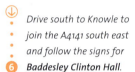

Backtrack a little to pick up the A452 south and turn onto the B4102 west to **Hampton in Arden**. ⑤

Drive south to Knowle to join the A4141 south east and follow the signs for **Baddesley Clinton Hall**. ⑥

3 COVENTRY

A wealthy medieval town and later the centre of the British motor industry, Coventry was a major target for German bombers during World War II. As a consequence, the city you see today is mostly modern. Its crowning glory is the graceful pink sandstone **St Michael's Cathedral**, designed by Sir Basil Spence and completed in 1962. This masterpiece of post-war construction has a soaring nave and wonderful stained glass by John Piper. A fascinating Graham Sutherland tapestry hangs above the altar, and at the entrance is a statue of St Michael defeating the devil by Sir Jacob Epstein. Beside the modern cathedral are the haunting remains of the original 14th-century St Michael's, destroyed in the bombings, whose spire still stands defiantly. In the summer you can climb to the top for wonderful views over the ruins and the city.

Nearby, the **Priory Visitor Centre** stands on the site of yet another cathedral – Coventry's first. This building, said to have held the tombs of Earl Leofric and Lady Godiva, was destroyed by Henry VIII in the early 1500s due to its monastic links. The ruins are now almost entirely below ground level, but it is possible to take a guided tour, and some of the finds from the recent excavation can be seen in the visitor centre. Another highlight is the **Herbert Art Gallery and Museum** with displays on local history, a Godiva room celebrating the city's most famous resident, and sculptures by Henry Moore and Barbara Hepworth.

Continue along the A4141 to join the A4177 north and then the A452 east to **Kenilworth Castle**.

→ • • • • • • • • • • • ⑦

4 NATIONAL MOTORCYCLE MUSEUM

Recognised as one of the biggest and best motorcycle museums in the world, the National Motorcycle Museum was rebuilt after a devastating fire in 2003 and now houses more than 650 restored motorbikes. It is a must if you are a classic bike enthusiast. It chronicles the golden years of British motorcycling, when locally made models were exported all over the world.

5 HAMPTON IN ARDEN

The sleepy village of Hampton in Arden has a host of 17th-century timber-framed buildings and a pretty 12th- to 15th-century church with a picturesque graveyard. Although there are no particular visitor attractions here, it is a pleasant place to stop for a stroll along the River Blythe to the 13th-century packhorse bridge.

6 BADDESLEY CLINTON HALL

Baddesley Clinton Hall is a unique and beautiful medieval moated manor house famous as a refuge for Catholic priests during the late 16th century. Three priest holes can still be seen here, as well as the timber-framed Great Hall, copious armorial glass and an enchanting 19th-century chapel. The house is maintained in typical Elizabethan style – in fact, little has changed since the death of its most influential owner, the wealthy Squire Henry Ferrers, in 1633. The house is surrounded by gardens, with a beautiful lake walk and nature trail, and nearby you can access the historic Grand Union Canal at Kingswood.

LADY GODIVA

Lady Godiva, the wife of wealthy Lord Leofric, Earl of Mercia, was a patron of the arts in the early 11th century. Aware that the people of Coventry could not afford to think about lofty artistic ideals while struggling to keep food on the table, she pleaded with her husband to reduce the taxes paid by the poor. He eventually relented on condition that she ride around the town naked. To his immense surprise, she agreed, forcing him to eliminate the taxes. A later, more puritanical, version of the story says she ordered all townsfolk to stay indoors as she rode through town; only one, the original Peeping Tom, dared look at her – and he was struck blind as a result.

7 KENILWORTH CASTLE

The spectacular ruins of Kenilworth Castle were made famous by Sir Walter Scott's novel *Kenilworth* in 1862, and have been an inspiration to writers from J R R Tolkien to J K Rowling. The castle was begun in the early 12th century, and its sturdy Norman keep still stands firm in spite of years of attack and siege. Kenilworth was an important Midlands stronghold and was heavily fortified in the 14th and 16th centuries, surrounded by a massive artificial lake and given enormous curtain walls. Later, under the ownership of John of Gaunt and Robert Dudley, the castle was transformed into a palace. Dudley spent much of his wealth entertaining Elizabeth I with extravagant parties and performances here. Today, the audio tour brings the castle ruins to life and recounts the tales of its many battles and royal visits .

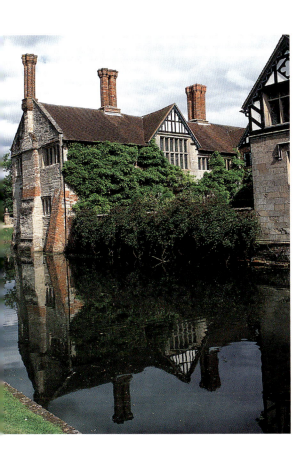

Clockwise from far left:
the old St Michael's Cathedral, Coventry; Kenilworth Castle; Baddesley Clinton Hall; the tapestry above the altar in the new St Michael's Cathedral, Coventry

8 STONELEIGH ABBEY

The Cistercian abbey at Stoneleigh was begun in 1154, but the property was much altered over the years and eventually became the home of the Leigh family in 1561. The charming 14th-century gatehouse is one of the oldest parts of the property to survive, but most of the building that stands here today dates from the Georgian period. The grand Palladian west wing with its elaborate plaster ceilings was completed in 1726, while the Banqueting Hall is a wonderful example of Gothic Revival architecture. Over the years many famous faces have stayed at Stoneleigh – including Jane Austen, a relative of the Leigh family, who used her visits as inspiration for parts of *Persuasion* and *Mansfield Park*. The house is surrounded by a vast landscaped estate and is a wonderful place for leisurely walking.

*Take the A452 south east to join the B4115 north and follow the signs for **Stoneleigh Abbey**.* 8

*Backtrack to the A452 and follow it south east into **Royal Leamington Spa**.* 1

WITH MORE TIME

Whether you're a classic car buff or just have a vague interest, the **Heritage Motor Centre** *(left)* in Gaydon does a great job of tracing the history of the British automobile industry and the social changes it has brought about. The museum is home to the largest collection of classic and vintage British cars in the world, and has restored models dating from 1896 right up to the latest Aston Martin. Displays on how cars, roads and motoring have evolved bring the past to life, as does the fully restored 1930s garage. You can also watch archive films in an Art Deco cinema.

Worcestershire: land of hope and glory

Rows of undulating hills sweep right across the county of Worcestershire, birthplace of composer Edward Elgar and setting for the long-running BBC radio show *The Archers*. This is a county brimming with ecclesiastical architecture, from the glorious cathedral in the county capital to the dignified old abbey churches of Tewkesbury and Great Malvern. But far more than just a place of peace and worship, Worcestershire is also a region steeped in history: witness to bloody battles and full of brine baths, beautiful gardens and spectacular ruins. Take to the hills for some uplifting walks with sweeping vistas over the plains below.

TOUR ROUTE

Worcester ①
Spetchley Park and Gardens ②
Pershore ③
Tewkesbury ④
Upton upon Severn ⑤
Great Malvern ⑥
Lower Brockhampton House ⑦
Witley Court ⑧
Hartlebury Castle ⑨
Harvington Hall ⑩
Droitwich ⑪

TOUR LENGTH

DISTANCE approx. 100 miles (160km)
DURATION 3 days

TOURIST INFORMATION CENTRES

DROITWICH St Richard's House, Victoria Square, WR9 8DS; 01905 774312

GREAT MALVERN 21 Church Street, WR14 2AA; 01684 892289

WORCESTER The Guildhall, High Street, WR1 2EY; 01905 726311

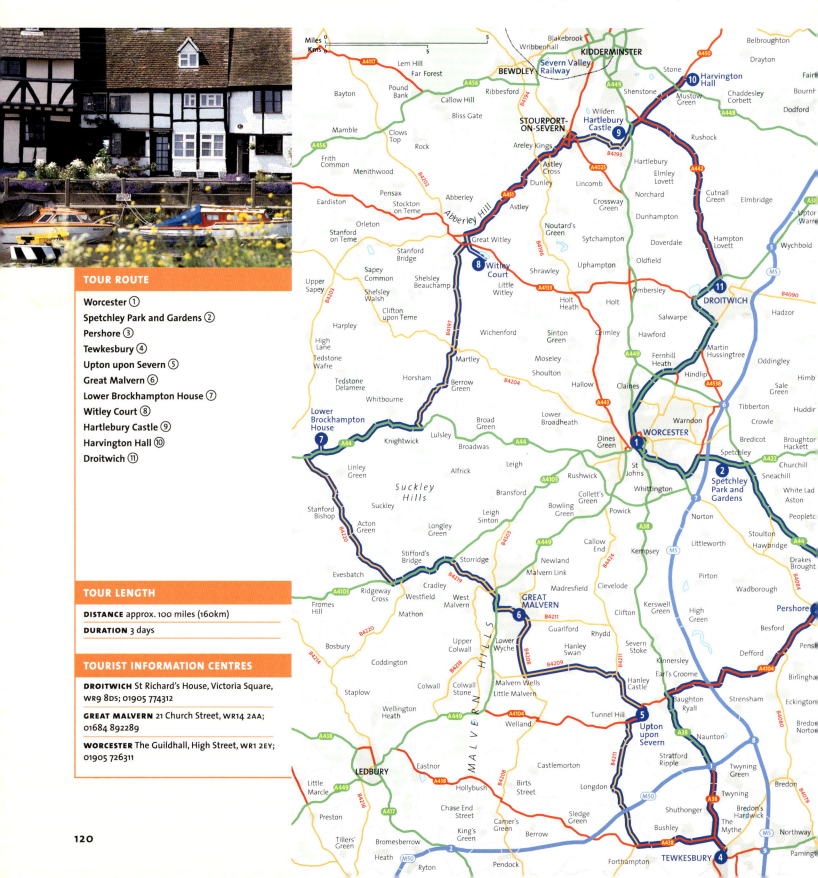

Clockwise from far left:
Tudor buildings along
Tewkesbury's riverside; the
Malvern Hills; Worcester
Cathedral; a statue at the
Greyfriars in Worcester

1 WORCESTER

The county town of Worcester makes a great base from which to tour the surrounding area and discover its long and turbulent history. Its main attraction is, of course, the lofty **cathedral**, begun in 1084 but much altered over the years to create the present glorious showcase of architectural styles. The sturdy nave is largely Norman, although embellished with Victorian stained glass windows, while the delicate choir and Lady Chapel are beautifully wrought in 13th-century Early English style. In the choir you'll find the tomb of King John, England's most-hated monarch, who was buried here in 1216. Below the cathedral is the largest Norman crypt in the country, while impressive cloisters and the circular 12th-century chapter house are found to its south.

A short walk away, Friar Street is lined with pretty Tudor and Elizabethan buildings, but the big draw here is the **Greyfriars**, a restored merchant's house dating from 1480. In addition to a lovely collection of textiles and furniture, it has a gorgeous walled garden at the back. Further down on New Street you'll find **King Charles House**, famous as the place where King Charles II escaped through a back door after his defeat in the Battle of Worcester, while on the High Street the Queen Anne-style **guildhall** is also worth a look for its fantastic period decoration.

To the south of the cathedral grounds, the **Commandery** occupies a Tudor building that was used as Charles II's headquarters in the run up to the Battle of Worcester in 1651; the exhibits inside chronicle those turbulent times. Just opposite is the **Royal Worcester** porcelain works, which has been producing fine china since 1751. It has an interesting visitor centre and museum charting the history of the company and its wares.

To see the city from a different angle, take a cruise along the River Severn, or alternatively stroll the paths along its banks. Just outside town, Worcester's most famous son, Edward Elgar *(see p123)*, is commemorated at the modest cottage where he was born in 1757. The **Elgar Birthplace Museum** contains a variety of the composer's personal effects, plus rare manuscripts, musical scores and photographs. There are also opportunities for visitors to listen to Elgar's music.

Drive east from Worcester
on the A422 to reach
Spetchley Park and Gardens.

 • • • • • • • • • • **2**

Continue east to pick up the A44 south east, then turn right onto the A4104 to Pershore.

3

Drive south west on the A4104 to join the A38 south to Tewkesbury.

4

Head west on the A438, then north on the B4211 to Upton upon Severn.

5

2 SPETCHLEY PARK AND GARDENS

The gorgeous park at Spetchley surrounds an imposing Georgian mansion that is home to the Berkeley family. Successive generations of Berkeleys have gathered and nurtured exotic species from around the globe to create a landscape full of rare plants, shrubs and trees. Formal Victorian gardens sit comfortably alongside mysterious woods and expansive parkland complete with its own herds of red and fallow deer.

3 PERSHORE

The charming Georgian town of Pershore boasts an atmospheric medieval **abbey** with a turbulent past. Most of the abbey you see today dates from the 13th century, and although much reduced from its former splendour (only the choir and transept of the original church remain) it has some wonderful ploughshare vaulting and an impressive pinnacled tower. The streets surrounding the abbey are thick with listed Georgian buildings and are a good place to wander, while just out of town is the mostly medieval **Pershore Bridge**, scene of many skirmishes during the Civil War.

4 TEWKESBURY

Tudor Tewkesbury missed out on the boom of the Industrial Revolution, so many of its crooked medieval houses, stately Georgian homes and lovely riverside warehouses have survived intact. Church Street and Mill Street are lined with warped old timber-framed buildings, but the town's crowning glory is the massive **abbey church** of St Mary the Virgin. Built on the site of a previous Saxon church, the Norman abbey was begun in 1092 and was given a further makeover in the 14th century. However, it was only by scrimping and saving that the townspeople managed to keep the church from destruction at the time of the Dissolution. They paid Henry VIII the princely sum of £453 to keep it as a spectacular parish church. The massive edifice has the largest Norman tower in the world and features magnificent ribbed and vaulted ceilings, fascinating tombs and dazzling 14th-century stained glass. Just south west of the abbey, off Lincoln Green Lane, is the site of the 1471 Battle of Tewkesbury, one of the defining battles of the War of the Roses.

Clockwise from above:
view of a reservoir in the
Malvern Hills; St Ann's Well,
Great Malvern; the river and
town at Tewkesbury

ELGAR AND THE MALVERN HILLS

Sir Edward Elgar *(below)*, perhaps best known as the composer of the score for *Land of Hope and Glory*, often claimed that the rolling Malvern Hills were the inspiration for his music. Born at Lower Broadheath, just outside Worcester, he lived in both Great Malvern and Malvern Link and frequently took to the hills both on foot and by bicycle, letting tunes form in his head as he went. During his 13 years in the area he wrote some of his finest music, telling friends, 'music is in the air all around you, you just take as much of it as you want'. You can follow in the composer's footsteps on the Elgar Trail, a circular driving or cycling route that takes you past the places most important in Elgar's life and music.

5 UPTON UPON SEVERN

Upton upon Severn is a lovely town of meandering narrow streets flanked by Tudor and Georgian houses. In its oldest building, known as The Pepperpot, the **heritage centre** charts local history, while nearby the **Tudor House** has displays on life in times past. The town is also justly famous for the Upton Jazz Festival, which attracts a host of international acts every June.

6 GREAT MALVERN

The Victorians flocked to Great Malvern to take advantage of the medicinal waters spurting from the steep hillside on which the town is built. Today their legacy remains in the elegant streets lined with fine houses and the genteel air that emanates from the town. You can still take the waters at the beautifully carved **St Ann's Well** high up on the hill, or enhance your health by rambling through the **Malvern Hills**, which rise steeply from the plains below with stunning views in all directions. Back in the town, you can get the low-down on Victorian medicinal practices at the Malvern Town Museum, situated in the gatehouse of the impressive **Great Malvern Priory**. This Benedictine priory, begun in 1085, is a showcase of Norman and Perpendicular style with a series of fascinating misericords and some extraordinary medieval stained glass. The town is also home to the **Malvern Theatres**, which host a lively programme of events.

Continue on the B4211 to
Hanley Castle, then take
the B4209 and the B4208
to Great Malvern. **6**

Head out of town on the
B4219 to join the A4103
west, then after 2 miles
turn north on the B4220.
When you reach the A44
turn right and then left to
reach Lower Brockhampton.

 **7**

*Backtrack to the A44 and
drive east to pick up the
B4197 to Great Witley, from
where you can follow signs
for **Witley Court**.*

7 LOWER BROCKHAMPTON HOUSE

Deeply romantic Lower Brockhampton House is a
14th-century half-timbered manor house surrounded
by a moat and set deep in a wooded valley. The
higgledy-piggledy building stands at the heart of
a 690-ha (1700-acre) estate and is protected by a
crooked half-timbered gatehouse that straddles the
moat. Nearby is a striking ruined Norman chapel,
and surrounding all are ancient woodlands that
make for excellent walking.

8 WITLEY COURT

The spectacular ruins of Witley Court, an extravagant 19th-century mansion, are a breathtaking sight rising from the magnificent landscaped gardens. In 1846 William Humble Ward, the first Earl of Dudley, began work to convert the early Jacobean manor house here into a sumptuous Italianate palace, but less than 100 years later a tragic fire devastated the house. Today, the atmospheric ruins are eerily empty but have lost none of their monumental scale.

While you're here, make sure to visit the parish church in nearby **Great Witley**. Though a rather plain structure on the outside, the interior is a Baroque masterpiece bursting with exuberance.

9 HARTLEBURY CASTLE

Home to the bishops of Worcester for over 1,000 years, Hartlebury Castle began life as a more humble manor house. Work to convert the house to the castle you see today began in 1255, but the structure was damaged during the Civil War. Most of the building now dates from the late 15th century, with 17th- and 18th-century Gothic additions. It is now home to the **Worcestershire County Museum**, which displays artefacts from Roman times to the 20th century and provides a wonderful insight into life in Worcestershire in times past.

10 HARVINGTON HALL

The moated medieval manor house at Harvington was updated and expanded during the late 16th century – a time when it was considered high treason for a Catholic priest to be in England. For this reason, Catholic owner Humphrey Pakington had a series of fascinating priest-holes built into the structure to help hide visiting clerics. Many of the rooms feature original Elizabethan wall paintings, and the Georgian chapel comes complete with 18th-century altar, rails and organ. Also in the grounds are an Elizabethan malt-house with an 18th-century malting kiln and a well-restored herb garden.

11 DROITWICH

Droitwich was famous for its massive salt deposits in Roman times and over the years the town grew rich on the back of the trade in that commodity. Even today, the wonderful collection of medieval buildings and fine merchant houses lining the streets indicates the great wealth brought here by the salt industry – look out for the timber-framed Elizabethan **Raven Hotel** and the beautifully restored **Priory House**. When the salt industry fell into decline during the 19th century, Droitwich successfully transformed itself into a spa town, opening brine baths and a brine-filled lido for the treatment of various ailments. The **Droitwich Spa Heritage Centre** does a good job of explaining the history of the town and illustrates how many of its buildings suffered from subsidence caused by salt mining.

*Head back to Great Witley and take the A451 north east to Stourport-on-Severn, from where you can take the B4193 to **Hartlebury Castle**.* **9**

*Drive north east, crossing the A449 to pick up the A450 to **Harvington Hall**.* **10**

*Backtrack on the A450 to the A442 and follow it south to **Droitwich**.* **11**

*Take the A38 south from Droitwich to **Worcester**.* **1**

WITH MORE TIME

The historic **Severn Valley Railway** *(left)* chugs for 16 glorious miles down the Severn Valley from Bridgnorth to Kidderminster, following the river closely and passing over six viaducts and the Victoria Bridge, a massive single-span structure high above the river. Steam-hauled passenger trains run the route every weekend (daily during holiday periods), and with few roads to spoil the views of the undulating countryside it makes a fantastic old-world day out. You can stop off at any of the charming traditional stations en route to explore local villages or take riverside walks.

Herefordshire's black-and-white villages and the Golden Valley

Rolling hills give way to lush green fields and sleepy cider orchards in rural Herefordshire, a rustic idyll that seems far from the beaten track. The River Wye flows gently past Hereford's imposing cathedral, through second-hand book mecca Hay-on-Wye, and on to the Welsh border. Little-visited and unspoilt by commercial attractions, this area is ideal for leisurely drives along glorious valleys and through picturesque villages.

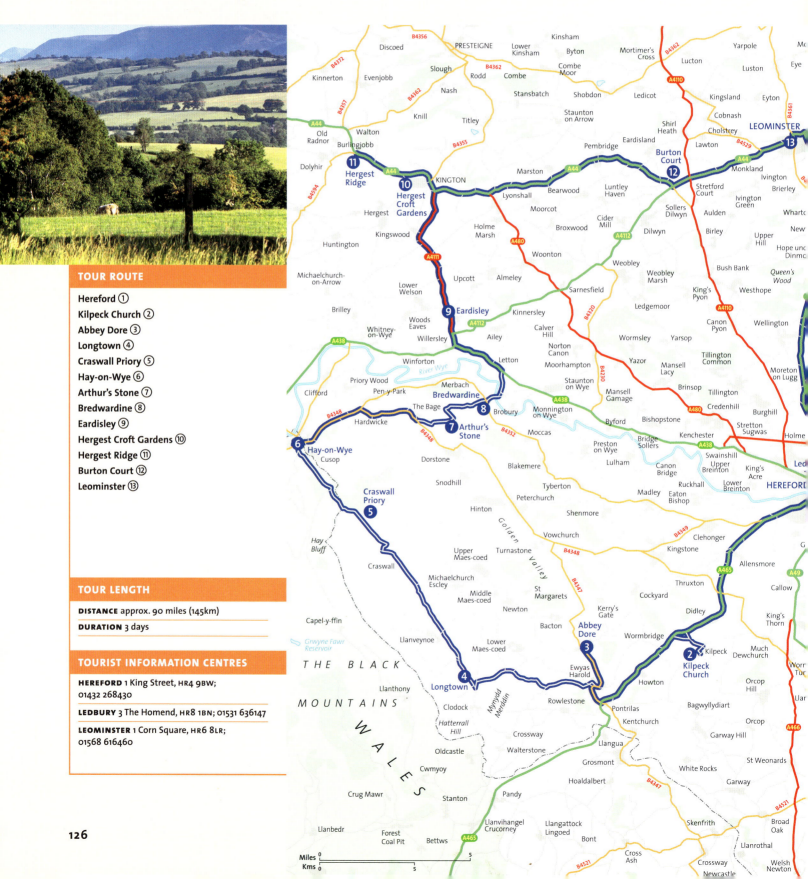

TOUR ROUTE

Hereford ①
Kilpeck Church ②
Abbey Dore ③
Longtown ④
Craswall Priory ⑤
Hay-on-Wye ⑥
Arthur's Stone ⑦
Bredwardine ⑧
Eardisley ⑨
Hergest Croft Gardens ⑩
Hergest Ridge ⑪
Burton Court ⑫
Leominster ⑬

TOUR LENGTH

DISTANCE approx. 90 miles (145km)

DURATION 3 days

TOURIST INFORMATION CENTRES

HEREFORD 1 King Street, HR4 9BW; 01432 268430

LEDBURY 3 The Homend, HR8 1BN; 01531 636147

LEOMINSTER 1 Corn Square, HR6 8LR; 01568 616460

Clockwise from far left:
Golden Valley; countryside around Hay-on-Wye; wood carving, Hereford Cathedral; Hereford Cider Museum and King Offa Distillery; carvings, Kilpeck Church

1 HEREFORD

Languid county capital and centre of the region's agricultural and cider industries, Hereford is a curious place with an old-fashioned feel and some unusual attractions. Topping the bill is its small-scale **cathedral**, a showcase of architectural styles from the sturdy Norman nave and the stunning 13th-century Lady Chapel through to the 14th-century choir and the grand Victorian choir screen, a Gothic Revival masterpiece. The cathedral's main claim to fame, however, is the remarkable **Mappa Mundi**, a geographical, mythological and historical map of the world as it was understood by cartographers in 1290. In the same building you'll also find the chained library – the largest example in the world – which boasts tomes dating back to the 8th century, still secured to the shelves with their original locks and chains.

From the cathedral it's just a short walk to the **Old House**, a half-timbered Jacobean building on the main square. The house dates from 1621, and inside the rooms have been refurbished in period style. Also worth a look are the **Hereford Museum and Art Gallery**, which has a collection of Roman artefacts including some beautiful mosaics, and the **Hereford Cider Museum and King Offa Distillery**, a reconstructed cider farmhouse and working distillery that explains the history and production of the local brew, and also offers tastings.

*From Hereford, drive south west on the A465 for 8 miles, then turn left and follow the signs for **Kilpeck Church**.* **2**

2 KILPECK CHURCH

The diminutive Norman church at Kilpeck is a remarkable place, almost perfectly preserved and left largely untouched since its completion around the middle of the 12th century. It is famous for its extraordinary carvings, most of which are organic, rather than Christian symbols. Celtic, Nordic and even Oriental influences can be traced in the red sandstone figures, the most sexually explicit of which were removed by the prudish Victorians. The Sheela-na-Gig, a Celtic fertility symbol, still survives, as do a wonderful Tree of Life and more than 70 grotesques.

*Backtrack to the A465 and continue south before turning right onto the B4347 to **Abbey Dore**.*

 **3**

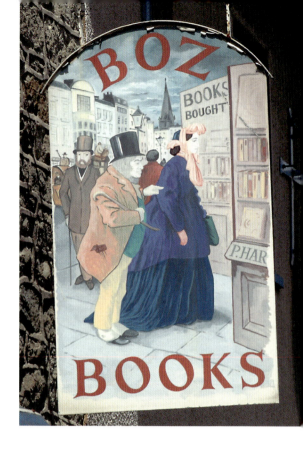

*Backtrack on the B4347
to Ewyas Harold, then turn
right onto a minor road*
4 *to Longtown.*

3 ABBEY DORE

Nestled in the beautiful Golden Valley, where rolling green hills and heather-covered ridges sweep down from the Black Mountains, the village of Abbey Dore is a historic place and home to the remains of the fine Cistercian **Dore Abbey**. Founded in 1147, the abbey was dissolved and largely destroyed in 1536, but the chancel and transept of its church survived and were restored in the 17th century to be used as the parish church. Many fine features remain from both periods, including medieval floor tiles and bosses, a musician's gallery and a Renaissance screen. Also worth a look is **Abbey Dore Court Garden**, a rambling open space that mixes formality and fun along the banks of the River Dore.

4 LONGTOWN

The sleepy village of Longtown is home to the ruins of a dramatic **castle** built by Norman lords in an attempt to control the wily Welsh. The motte-and-bailey castle is set in the foothills of the Black Mountains and originates from the 1180s. In the 13th century it was fortified with a twin-towered gatehouse, a portcullis and a round keep with 5m-thick walls (15ft), the remains of which can be clearly identified today. Surrounding the castle itself are the remnants of a medieval town created to help colonise the border area. By the 14th century, the castle had begun to decay and was abandoned, but it saw a brief burst of life in the early 15th century when Owain Glyndwr led a rebellion to reclaim land lost to the English.

Driving between Longtown and Hay you pass through the foothills of the Black Mountains, home to some glorious scenery and a dramatic backdrop for the drive. Cresting the ridge of the mountains is Offa's Dyke Path *(see p107)*, a long-distance walking trail from Chepstow to Prestatyn, which follows the route of Offa's 8th-century earthworks.

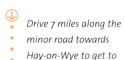
*Drive 7 miles along the
minor road towards
Hay-on-Wye to get to*
5 *Craswall Priory.*

5 CRASWALL PRIORY

The French Grandmont monks were the most austere monastic order of the Middle Ages, and they established their monastery at Craswall in the early 13th century. Only scant ruins remain, but these have been left all but untouched since the abbey was confiscated by the crown during the Hundred Years War.

*Continue north west on
minor roads from Craswall
to reach to Hay-on-Wye.*
 **6**

HEREFORDSHIRE'S CIDER ROUTE

The lush, fecund hills of this region are famed for their apple orchards, cultivated since the 17th century. Farmers began to produce cider to serve to their farm labourers during hay-making and harvest, and in the 1600s Lord Scudamore championed cider-making in the county as an industry in itself. Soon Herefordshire became known as the leading cider producer in England, and even today the world's largest cider mill, **Bulmers**, is located here. Sadly, the traditional orchards have been in decline for the last 60 years, with many rare apple varieties being lost as intensive farming methods take over. A wonderful way to see the old orchards before they disappear is to cycle the **cider route**, which meanders along quiet, scenic lanes. You can pick up a copy of the tour from local tourist offices.

6   HAY-ON-WYE

Hay-on-Wye, the book capital of the world, is a sleepy kind of place full of second-hand bookshops and independently minded people. The town famously declared itself an autonomous region in 1977 when Richard Booth, local bookseller and self-proclaimed King of Hay, began his grand plan to rejuvenate the area. It worked: Hay now has a growing population and 39 bookshops, the largest of which is Booth's own in **Hay Castle**, a battered Jacobean mansion built into the remains of a 13th-century castle. The town bursts into life each May for the annual literary festival but is a pretty place year round, riddled with steep, narrow streets and set against the Black Mountains.

Clockwise from left:
bookshop sign, Hay-on-Wye;
Arthur's Stone

7   ARTHUR'S STONE

This ancient burial chamber near Dorstone supposedly marks the spot where King Arthur slew a giant and then buried him beneath the impressive 25-tonne capstone. The official line, however, is that the site is Neolithic, dating from about 3000BC, and would once have been covered by an earth mound. Just to the south is another stone, known locally as the Quoit Stone, which has two indentations. Local lore suggests that this was where Arthur placed his elbows when he prayed, or possibly where the giant left an imprint of his knees as he fell.

8   BREDWARDINE

The Victorian diarist, the Reverend Francis Kilvert, spent the last two years of his life as the vicar for Bredwardine and both he and his wife, Elizabeth are buried in the churchyard. His delightful diaries tell of the everyday life of many places and people in what is now called Kilvert Country. He often visited his sister, Thersie, who was married to the vicar of nearby Monnington on Wye; while Clyro, where he served as curate from 1865 to 1872, lies just beyond Hay-on-Wye.

*Leave Hay on the B4348 to Dorstone and follow the signs to the left for **Arthur's Stone**.* **7**

*Drive east on minor roads to reach **Bredwardine**.* **8**

*Travel north east, crossing the River Wye to pick up the A438 west and then the A4111 north into **Eardisley**.*   **9**

9 EARDISLEY

The pretty half-timbered village of Eardisley is home to the **Church of St Mary Magdalene**, famous for its red sandstone font. The font dates from the 12th century, and is richly carved with symbols similar to those at Kilpeck Church *(see p127)*. Outside, a beautifully restored lych gate marks the entrance to the churchyard. Nearby, the scant remains of Eardisley's motte-and-bailey **castle** can be seen. Once the home of Robert de Lacy, the castle burned down in the 13th century, and the grassy mound and moat stream are now all that is left to mark the spot.

Head north again on the A4111, then west on the A44, following signs to the left for
10 *Hergest Croft Gardens.*

10 HERGEST CROFT GARDENS

Three generations of the Banks family have presided over the creation of the stunning Hergest Croft Gardens near Kington. Surrounding an Edwardian house and offering wonderful views over the Black Mountains, the gardens are divided into four distinct sections. At the centre, magnolias, cherries and hydrangeas bloom, while the nearby kitchen garden has a collection of well-established apple trees, double herbaceous borders, and a wonderfully old-fashioned rose garden. Massive cedars, birches and maples dominate the azalea garden, while in Park Woods, hidden valleys and woodland glades cut between the ancient oak trees.

*Return to the A44 and drive west. Turn left onto the B4594 to reach the top of **Hergest Ridge**.*
11

BLACK-AND-WHITE VILLAGE TRAIL

A cluster of gorgeous black-and-white Tudor villages just west of Leominster have survived the centuries intact and are now the setting for one of the most idyllic drives in the county. The **Black-and-White Village Trail** is a 40-mile circular route taking you back in time to traditional villages where half-timbered houses and quaint churches huddle round village greens. **Pembridge** has a black-and-white villages centre with information on the whole area, as well as a lovely church and bell tower, and an old market hall. Nearby, riverside **Eardisland** *(below)* is probably the most picturesque of all, with undulating roofs, rickety cottages and a meandering brook.

Clockwise from above:
two views of Hergest Croft
Gardens; half-timbered
building in Leominster;
house in Eardisley

11 HERGEST RIDGE

Made famous by Mike Oldfield's chart-topping album, Hergest Ridge is a gorgeously green hill rising gently over the Welsh border from Kington. You can drive across the ridge, or alternatively join Offa's Dyke Path *(see p107)* at Hergest Croft Gardens and walk up for beautiful views over the surrounding area.

12 BURTON COURT

Burton Court is one of Herefordshire's finest squire's houses, with wonderful Regency and Victorian rooms and an original 14th-century Great Hall. The house was built on the site of an ancient camp, supposedly where the future Henry V stationed troops to watch over Owain Glyndwr. You can visit the house and gardens, pick your own fruit in season, and even stay in the holiday accommodation in the north wing.

13 LEOMINSTER

The historic Welsh borders town of Leominster thrived on the wool trade in medieval times, and the pretty half-timbered houses from that era still give the town its character today. This is a sleepy place with a bevy of antiques shops, but it also boasts an unusually wide **priory church**, with a remarkable double nave. The church retains some original Norman features as well as some stunning Gothic characteristics (look out for the Green Man fertility symbol on the west door) and one of England's last remaining ducking stools.

Backtrack to Kington, then
drive 8 miles east on the
A44 and follow the signs
*for **Burton Court**.* **12**

Continue east along
the A44 to reach
***Leominster**.* **13**

Drive south on the A49
*back to **Hereford**.*
1

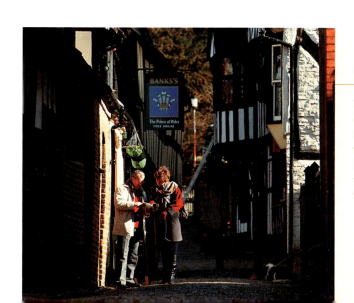

WITH MORE TIME

The narrow lanes, Tudor architecture and excellent antiques shops make **Ledbury** *(left)* well worth the trip. The first stop in the town centre is the Market House, a herringbone-patterned Tudor hall perched high on oak legs. Nearby, Church Lane is flanked with atmospheric Tudor and Stuart houses and home to the Butcher's Row House Museum with its displays on local history, plus the magnificent Painted Room with its collection of 16th-century floral frescoes. Finally, visit the largely Norman St Michael's Parish Church to marvel at its soaring spire and elaborate tombs.

Shropshire: birthplace of the Industrial Revolution

Despite its well-preserved Tudor towns, rolling blue-remembered hills, world-famous industrial heritage and glorious gourmet cuisine, sparsely populated Shropshire still attracts only a trickle of visitors. Consequently, those who do make it here are rewarded with unspoilt countryside, authentic attractions and the effortlessly easy nature of locals genuinely glad to see you.

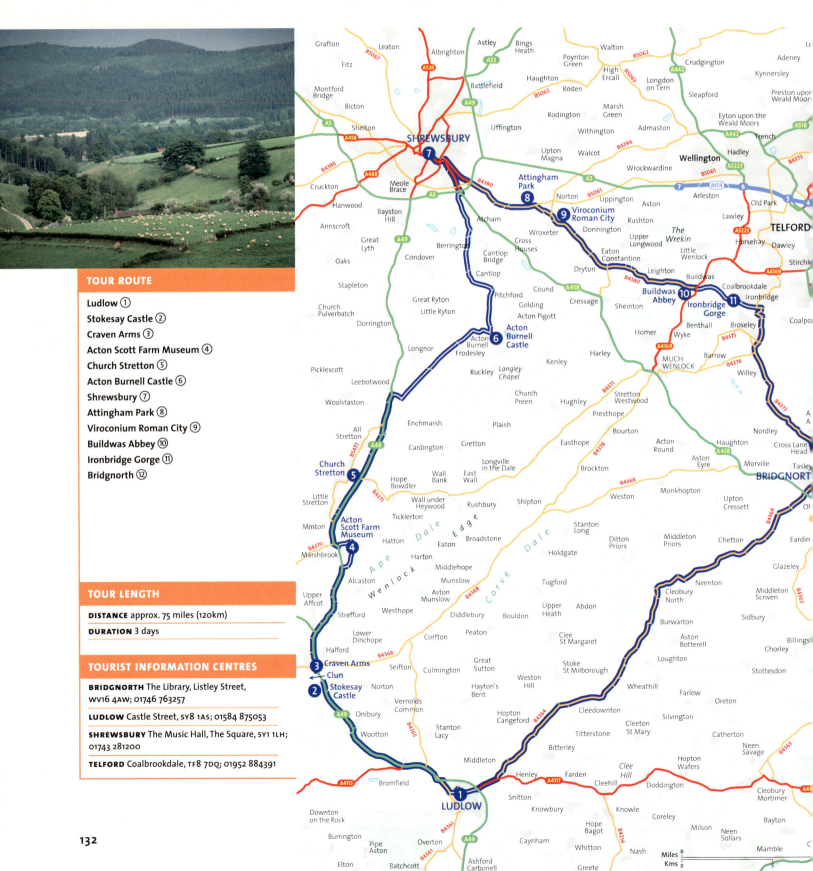

TOUR ROUTE

Ludlow ①
Stokesay Castle ②
Craven Arms ③
Acton Scott Farm Museum ④
Church Stretton ⑤
Acton Burnell Castle ⑥
Shrewsbury ⑦
Attingham Park ⑧
Viroconium Roman City ⑨
Buildwas Abbey ⑩
Ironbridge Gorge ⑪
Bridgnorth ⑫

TOUR LENGTH

DISTANCE approx. 75 miles (120km)
DURATION 3 days

TOURIST INFORMATION CENTRES

BRIDGNORTH The Library, Listley Street, WV16 4AW; 01746 763257
LUDLOW Castle Street, SY8 1AS; 01584 875053
SHREWSBURY The Music Hall, The Square, SY1 1LH; 01743 281200
TELFORD Coalbrookdale, TF8 7DQ; 01952 884391

Clockwise from far left:
landscape around Ludlow;
the castle and town,
Ludlow; street scene,
Ludlow; Ludlow Castle;
gatehouse, Stokesay Castle

1 LUDLOW

Listed black-and-white buildings, Georgian townhouses and Michelin-starred restaurants line the streets of Ludlow, Shropshire's finest town and a wonderful base for discovering the county. The town is perched on a hilltop, a perfect defensive position for **Ludlow Castle**, built by the Normans to keep control of the warring Welsh and targeted over the years in numerous attacks. The towers, turrets, keep and gatehouse survived the onslaught, and today the atmospheric ruins still maintain a dignified air. There's also a fascinating round chapel dating from 1120, and set into the castle walls is **Castle Lodge**, an Elizabethan mansion. Inside you'll find ornamental ceilings, oak-panelling, 14th-century fireplaces and an exhibition on the history of the town. Walking through Castle Square you'll reach the **Church of St Lawrence** with its marvellous stained glass windows and fascinating misericords. Nearby is the striking façade of the Feathers Hotel, a prime example of a Jacobean mansion. From here, you can follow the narrow, meandering lanes lined with speciality food shops, traditional butchers and cheesemongers to Broad Street, a sloping thoroughfare leading down to the River Teme and flanked by an elegant swathe of half-timbered houses and Georgian buildings. At the bottom stands the last of the town's original medieval gates.

*Drive north west from
Ludlow on the A49 and
follow the signs for
Stokesay Castle.* ②

2 STOKESAY CASTLE

England's wealthiest wool merchant, Lawrence of Ludlow, built Stokesay Castle in the late 13th century, during a period of relative peace in the area that allowed him to add such novel features as windows to his new home. The rather imposing fortified manor house was almost completely untouched over the years and has now been beautifully restored. The highlight is the Great Hall with its soaring ceiling and wonderfully carved Elizabethan fireplace, but a cluster of other interesting buildings huddle around the grassy courtyard, including a stunning timber-framed Jacobean gatehouse.

*Continue on the A49 for
one mile to **Craven Arms**.*

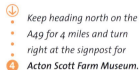

Keep heading north on the A49 for 4 miles and turn right at the signpost for **4** *Acton Scott Farm Museum.*

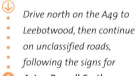

Return to the A49 and drive north to *Church* **5** *Stretton.*

Drive north on the A49 to Leebotwood, then continue on unclassified roads, following the signs for **6** *Acton Burnell Castle.*

Take minor roads north via Pitchford and Cantlop until you reach the A5 ringroad. From there, follow signs into the centre of *Shrewsbury.*

7

3 CRAVEN ARMS

The sleepy little market town of Craven Arms is worth a stop to visit the **Secret Hills Discovery Centre**, housed in an innovative, curving, grass-roofed building. Displays here examine the geology of the local landscape and explain how it evolved over the years. Other exhibits include a replica of the prehistoric Shropshire Mammoth and a simulated hot-air balloon flight.

4 ACTON SCOTT WORKING FARM MUSEUM

This historic working farm aims to demonstrate what rural life was like 100 years ago. Costumed guides drive teams of horses, make bread, struggle with washing, milk cows and make cheese daily, while a farrier, blacksmith and wheelwright give demonstrations weekly.

5 CHURCH STRETTON

Known to the Victorians as 'Little Switzerland', the area around the agreeable market town of Church Stretton is one of the most popular with Shropshire's walkers and ramblers. Rising to the west is the Long Mynd, a nine-mile ridge of upland heath, riddled with walking paths and scenic valleys. The **Carding Mill Valley Trail** is one of the most popular in the area, leading up to the National Trust-run **Chalet Pavilion** where there is a tearoom and information point. The trail starts just outside Church Stretton and meanders to the summit of the Long Mynd (518m, 1,700ft) where you'll get sweeping views across the plains to the Black Mountains.

6 ACTON BURNELL CASTLE

The isolated 13th-century fortified manor house at Acton Burnell was home to Robert Burnell, chancellor of England and a trusted friend of Edward I. The king visited Acton Burnell regularly, and the grand house was the site of the first English parliament at which the Commons was present. Today, only the evocative shell of the red sandstone building survives, but the location is beautiful. The attractive 13th-century Church of St Mary is close by the castle.

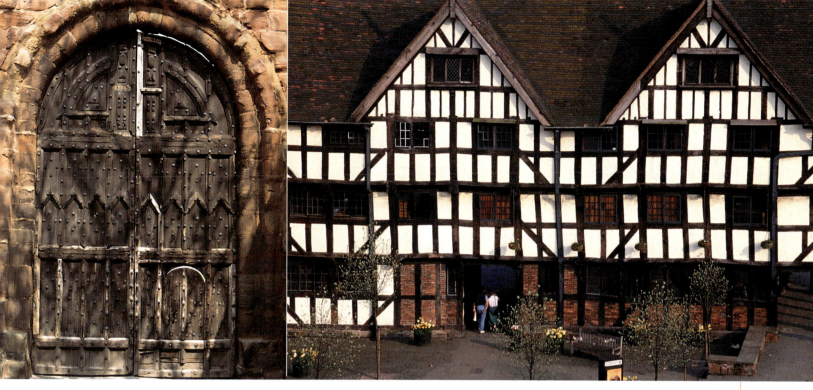

Clockwise from far left:
Hills near Church Stretton;
gateway, Shrewsbury Castle;
Rowley Mansion, Shrewsbury;
view of Shrewsbury;
Acton Burnell Castle

7 SHREWSBURY

Crooked, half-timbered buildings with rickety roofs line the meandering cobbled laneways of the Tudor heart of Shrewsbury, a laid-back place with a charming old-world atmosphere. Streets with such evocative names as Grope Lane, Butcher's Row and Fish Street have changed little since their overhanging black-and-white houses were built in medieval times. To wander the streets and discover such glories as the Abbot's House, Ireland's Mansion and the Bear Steps Hall is a sheer joy.

Shrewsbury is located within a loop of the meandering River Severn, and its strategic defensive position has made it an important centre since Saxon times. The Norman **castle** here was remodelled in the 14th century and again shored up, this time by Thomas Telford, in the 18th century. Today, it houses the **Shropshire Regimental Museum** with its vast collection of military memorabilia. Also worth a look is the **Shrewsbury Museum and Art Gallery** set in the lovely 16th- and 17th-century buildings known as Rowley's House. The museum displays the best of the finds unearthed at the nearby Roman city at Wroxeter *(see p136)*, plus exhibitions on the town's most famous sons, Charles Darwin and Robert Clive of India. Shrewsbury is also home to several picturesque churches: the Norman and Gothic St Mary's Church with its soaring spire and Jesse window; the round Georgian St Chad's lording it over the river; and the red sandstone Shrewsbury Abbey, a Norman church updated by the Victorians and home to some exquisite 14th-century stained glass.

8 ATTINGHAM PARK

Flamboyant Attingham Park was built by Noel Hill, the first Lord Berwick, who was eager to impress visitors and locals with his ostentatious wealth. The grandiose Georgian mansion has an imposing neoclassical façade and opulent Regency interiors filled with Italian furniture and over-the-top decor. A picture gallery by John Nash once housed a fine collection of Renaissance works, but the best of these were sold when the second lord lost the family fortune in the early 19th century. Outside the house, you can meander through the grounds, which were landscaped by Repton, following one of the woodland walks or the sculpture trail.

*Return south east to the A5 ring road and join the B4380 east, following the signs to **Atcham Park**.* **8**

*Continue east for 2 miles on the B4380 to Wroxeter and follow signs for **Viroconium Roman City**.*

 **9**

↓
Continue south east on the B4380 for 6 miles to Buildwas and follow signs
10 *to **Buildwas Abbey**.*

*Keep heading east on the minor road towards Ironbridge for **Ironbridge Gorge**.*

→ • • • • • • • • • • • **11**

9 VIROCONIUM ROMAN CITY

The Romans built their fourth largest city in Britain just outside present-day Wroxeter, at a strategic crossing point between the River Severn and Watling Street, an important Roman road. Almost 6,000 people lived here at one point, and although most of the ancient city remains are cloaked by farmland, the impressive bath complex can be visited. A modest on-site museum helps explain the significance and scale of the city.

10 BUILDWAS ABBEY

The atmospheric remains of Buildwas Abbey are largely unaltered since it was founded in the 12th century. Except for the roof, now missing, the monastery is remarkably intact: substantial parts are still standing including a fine Chapter House, a vaulted crypt, the cloisters and a sturdy Norman nave. Situated on the Welsh border, it had a turbulent history with frequent raids by unruly Welsh princes. It was eventually dissolved in 1535, following which it was incorporated into a private house. Buildwas is a stunning place to visit, its evocative ruins set against a backdrop of a wooded valley and surrounded by quiet meadows on the banks of the River Severn.

Clockwise from far left:
Iron Bridge, Ironbridge;
Blists Hill foundry,
Ironbridge; Roman remains,
Viroconium Roman City

11 IRONBRIDGE GORGE

Birthplace of the Industrial Revolution and home to the first iron bridge in the world, this wooded valley is now a World Heritage Site and a fascinating place to explore. The main village of Ironbridge tumbles prettily down the steep sides of the valley to the famous, 18th-century Iron Bridge. Here you'll find the **Museum of the Gorge**, which explains the history of the area and why it had such an influence on the world. In **Coalbrookdale** you can visit the original Darby houses, home to the famous family of engineers who revolutionised industrial processes, and see their iron foundry, now the engaging **Museum of Iron**. In all, there are ten museums in the area, ranging from the wonderfully restored **Coalport China Museum** to the open-air theme park of **Blists Hill Victorian Town** and the technology centre **Enginuity**.

12 BRIDGNORTH

The pretty town of Bridgnorth slithers down a steep cliff to the River Severn, half-timbered houses clinging doggedly to the hillside and a marvellous Victorian **cliff railway** transporting locals up and down the slope. The route runs from largely residential Low Town to High Town, where most visitor attractions are located. The views from High Town were described by King Charles I as 'the finest in my domain', and they are still impressive today. Also here is the wonderful 17th-century half-timbered Town Hall, the black-and-white shop fronts of the high street and a small local museum housed in the burly North Gate. At the far end of the high street is the delightful **St Mary's Church**, designed by Thomas Telford in 1794. Beside it you'll see a precariously leaning medieval tower, the final vestige of the town **castle**. Bridgnorth is also the northern terminus of the **Severn Valley Railway** *(see p125)*, which chugs placidly down the valley for 16 miles to Kidderminster.

Continue east to join
the B4373 south via
*Broseley to **Bridgnorth**.* 12

Follow the B4364 south
west from Bridgnorth to
*return to **Ludlow**.*
  1

THE WREKIN

The Wrekin is probably Shropshire's most famous landmark, and although only 396m (1,300ft) high, it rises so sharply from the low-lying land around it that it appears to be much taller. Numerous trails lead up the igneous hill and reward the walker with stunning views in all directions. Local folklore suggests that the Wrekin was the work of two giants who dug out the bed of the River Severn in order to build a base for a fortress.

WITH MORE TIME

The poet A E Housman famously described **Clun** as 'the quietest place under the sun', and little has changed since in this sleepy but charming village in the beautiful Clun Valley. The town is home to the impressive ruins of a Norman castle *(left)* built on a mound in a bend in the river. Also worth a look is the modest museum in the Town Hall and the Norman church of St George with its 18th-century lych gate. Nearby are the pretty 17th-century Trinity Almshouses, while to the west of town rise the uplands of Clun Forest, an excellent spot for walking.

Gazetteer

Norfolk: the essence of East Anglia

Blickling Hall, Garden and Park
Blickling, Norwich NR11 6NF
Tel: 01263 738030
www.nationaltrust.org.uk

Bure Valley Railway
Aylsham Station, Norwich Road,
Aylsham NR11 6RW
Tel: 01263 733814
www.bvrw.fsnet.co.uk

Caister Castle and Car Collection
Caister on Sea, Great Yarmouth
Tel: 01572 787251
www.greateryarmouth.co.uk

Holkham Hall
Wells-next-the-Sea NR23 1AB
Tel: 01328 710227
www.holkham.co.uk

Horsey Windpump
Horsey, Great Yarmouth NR29 4EF
Tel: 0870 609 5388
www.nationaltrust.org.uk

Houghton Hall
King's Lynn PE31 6UE
Tel: 01485 528569
www.houghtonhall.com

Mid Norfolk Railway
Dereham Station, Station Road,
Dereham NR19 1DF
Tel: 01362 690633
www.mnr.org.uk

The Muckleburgh Collection
Weybourne Military Camp, Weybourne NR25 7EG
Tel: 01263 588210
www.muckleburgh.co.uk

The Norfolk Motorcycle Museum
Rail Yard, North Walsham NR28 0DS
Tel: 01692 406266
www.northnorfolk.org

The Norfolk Nelson Museum
26 South Quay, Great Yarmouth NR30 2RG
Tel: 01493 850698
www.nelson-museum.co.uk

Norfolk Rural Life Museum
Gressenhall, Dereham NR20 4DR
Tel: 01362 860563
www.museums.norfolk.gov.uk

North Norfolk Railway
The Station, Sheringham NR26 8RA
Tel: 01263 820800
www.nnrailway.co.uk

Norwich Castle Museum and Art Gallery
Castle Meadow, Norwich NR1 3JU
Tel: 01603 493636
www.museums.norfolk.gov.uk

Norwich Cathedral
Norwich NR1 4EH
Tel: 01603 218320
www.cathedral.org.uk

RNLI Henry Blogg Museum
The Promenade, Cromer NR27 9HE
Tel: 01263 511294
www.cromerlifeboats.org.uk

Royal Norfolk Regimental Museum
Market Avenue, Norwich NR1 3JQ
Tel: 01603 493650
www.museums.norfolk.gov.uk

Sandringham Estate
Sandringham PE35 6EN
Tel: 01553 612908
www.sandringham-estate.co.uk

Sheringham Park
Upper Sheringham NR26 8TB
Tel: 01263 820550
www.nationaltrust.org.uk

Shirehall Museum
Common Place, Little Walsingham
NR22 6BP
Tel: 01328 820510

**Time and Tide Museum
of Great Yarmouth Life**
Blackfriars Road, Great Yarmouth
NR30 3BX
Tel: 01493 743930
www.museums.norfolk.gov.uk

Wells and Walsingham Railway
Wells-next-the-Sea NR 23 1QB
Tel: 01328 711630
www.wellswalsinghamrailway.co.uk

Marshes and muses: nature and art along the Suffolk coast

Adnams Brewery
Sole Bay Brewery, Southwold IP18 6JW
Tel: 01502 727200
www.adnams.co.uk

Africa Alive (Suffolk Wildlife Park)
White's Lane, Kessingland NR33 7TF
Tel: 01502 740291
www.suffolkwildlifepark.co.uk

Aldeburgh Museum, The Moot Hall
Moot Hall, Market Cross Place,
Aldeburgh IP15 5DS
Tel: 01728 454666
www.aldeburghmuseum.org.uk

Christchurch Mansion
Christchurch Park, Ipswich IP4 2BE
Tel: 01473 433554
www.ipswich.gov.uk

East Anglia Transport Museum
Chapel Road, Carlton Colville NR33 8BL
Tel: 01502 518459
www.eatm.org.uk

Framlingham Castle
Framlingham, Woodbridge IP13 9BP
Tel: 01728 724189
www.englishheritage.org.uk

Lowestoft Maritime Museum
Whapload Road, Lowestoft NR32 1XG
Tel: 01502 561963
www.aboutnorfolksuffolk.co.uk

Orford Castle
Orford, Woodbridge IP12 2ND
Tel: 01394 450472
www.english-heritage.org.uk

Parham Airfield Museum
Parham, Framlingham IP13 9AF
Tel: 01728 621373
www.parhamairfieldmuseum.co.uk

Saxmundham Museum
49 High Street, Saxmundham
IP17 1AJ
Tel: 01728 602341
www.saxmundham.org

Saxtead Green Post Mill
The Mill House, Saxtead Green,
Saxtead, Woodbridge IP13 9QQ
Tel: 01728 685789
www.english-heritage.org.uk

Snape Maltings
nr Saxmundham, Suffolk IP17 1SR
Tel: 01728 688303
www.snapemaltings.co.uk

Thorpeness Windmill Visitor Centre
Uplands Road, Thorpeness
Leiston IP16 4NQ
Tel: 01394 384948
www.suffolkcoastsandheaths.org

Woodbridge Tide Mill
Tide Mill Way, Woodbridge IP12 1AP
Tel: 01473 626618
www.tidemill.org.uk

Treasures of rural Suffolk

Grimes Graves
Lynford, Thetford IP26 5E
Tel: 01842 810656
www.english-heritage.org.uk

Ickworth House, Park and Garden
Ickworth, The Rotunda,
Horringer IP29 5QE
Tel: 01284 735270
www.nationaltrust.org.uk

Gainsborough's House
46 Gainsborough Street,
Sudbury CO10 2EU
Tel: 01787 372958
www.gainsborough.org

Kentwell Hall
Long Melford CO10 9BA
Tel: 01787 310207
www.kentwell.co.uk

Lavenham Guildhall
Market Place, Lavenham CO10 9QZ
Tel: 01787 247646
www.nationaltrust.org.uk

Lynford Arboretum
East Anglia Forest District,
Santon Downham, Brandon IP27 0TJ
Tel: 01842 810271
www.forestry.gov.uk

Manor House Museum
Honey Hill, Bury St Edmunds IP33 1RT
Tel: 01284 757076
www.stedmundsbury.gov.uk

Moyse's Hall Museum
Cornhill, Bury St Edmunds IP33 1DX
Tel: 01284 706183
www.stedmundsbury.gov.uk

Museum of East Anglian Life
Stowmarket IP14 1DL
Tel: 01449 612229
www.eastanglianlife.org.uk

The National Horseracing Museum
99 High Street, Newmarket CB8 8JL
Tel: 01638 667333
www.nhrm.co.uk

The National Stud
Newmarket CB8 0XE
Tel: 01638 666789
www.nationalstud.co.uk

Redwings Horse Sanctuary
Hapton, Norwich NR15 1SP
Tel: 01508 481000
www.redwings.org.uk

St Edmundsbury Cathedral
Bury St Edmunds IP33 1LS
Tel: 01284 754933
www.stedscathedral.co.uk

**West Stow Country Park and
Anglo-Saxon Village**
The Visitor Centre, Icklingham Road,
West Stow, Bury St Edmunds IP28 6HG
Tel: 01284 728718
www.stedmundsbury.gov.uk

The pleasant charms of Essex

Audley End House and Gardens
Saffron Walden CB11 4JF
Tel: 01799 522399
www.english-heritage.org.uk

Colchester Castle Museum
Castle Park, Colchester CO1 1TJ
Tel: 01206 282939
www.colchestermuseums.org.uk

Colchester Zoo
Maldon Road, Stanway, Colchester CO3 0SL
Tel: 01206 331292
www.colchester-zoo.com

Colne Valley Railway
Castle Hedingham CO9 3DZ
Tel: 01787 461174
www.colnevalleyrailway.co.uk

firstsite (relocating 2007)
The Minories Art Gallery,
74 High Street, Colchester CO1 1UE
Tel: 01206 577067
www.visitcolchester.co.uk

Flatford: Bridge Cottage
Flatford, East Bergholt CO7 6UL
Tel: 01206 298260
www.nationaltrust.org.uk

Hedingham Castle
Castle Hedingham CO9 3DJ
Tel: 01787 460261
www.hedinghamcastle.co.uk

Hollytrees Museum
High Street, Colchester CO1 1UG
Tel: 01206 282940
www.colchestermuseums.org.uk

House on the Hill Museum Adventure
Stansted Mountfitchet CM24 8SP
Tel: 01279 813567
www.hertsdirect.org

John Webb's Windmill
Thaxted
Tel: 01371 830285
www.thisisessex.co.uk

**Mountfitchet Castle
and Norman Village**
Stansted Mountfitchet CN24 8SP
Tel: 01279 813237
www.mountfitchetcastle.com

Tymperleys Clock Museum
Trinity Street, Colchester CO1 1JN
Tel: 01206 282943
www.colchestermuseums.org.uk

Hertfordshire's houses and gardens

Benington Lordship Gardens
Benington, Stevenage SG2 7BS
Tel: 08701 261709
www.beningtonlordship.co.uk

**Cathedral and Abbey Church
of St Alban**
St Albans AL1 1BY
Tel: 01727 860780
www.stalbanscathedral.org.uk

de Havilland Aircraft Heritage Centre
Salisbury Hall, London Colney AL2 1EX
Tel: 01727 822051
www.dehavillandmuseum.co.uk

**Dunstable Downs, Countryside
Centre and Whipsnade Estate**
Whipsnade Road, Kensworth,
Dunstable LU6 2TA
Tel: 01582 608489
www.nationaltrust.org.uk

The Gardens of the Rose
Chiswell Green, St Albans AL2 3NR
Tel: 01727 850461
www.rnrs.org

Hatfield House
Hatfield AL9 5NQ
Tel: 01707 287010
www.hatfield-house.co.uk

The Henry Moore Foundation
Dane Tree House, Perry Green,
Much Hadham SG10 6EE
Tel: 01279 843333
www.henry-moore-fdn.co.uk

Knebworth House
Knebworth SG3 6PY
Tel: 01438 812661
www.knebworthhouse.com

Medieval Clocktower
Market Place, St Albans AL1 5DJ
Tel: 01727 819340
www.stalbansmuseums.org.uk

Mill Green Museum
Mill Green, Hatfield AL9 5PD
Tel: 01707 271362
www.hertsmuseums.org.uk

Museum of St Albans
Hatfield Road, St Albans AL1 3RR
Tel: 01727 819340
www.stalbansmuseums.org.uk

The Roman Theatre of Verulamium
Bluehouse Hill, St Albans AL3 6AE
Tel: 01727 835035
www.romantheatre.co.uk

Scott's Grotto
28-34 Scotts Road, Ware SG12 9JN
Tel: 01920 464131
www.scotts-grotto.org

Shaw's Corner
Ayot St Lawrence, nr Welwyn AL6 9BX
Tel: 01494 755567
www.nationaltrust.org.uk

Stockwood Craft Museum and Gardens and Mossman Collection
Stockwood Park, Farley Hill, Luton LB1 4UH
Tel: 01582 738714
www.hertfordshire.co.uk

Verulamium Museum and Hypocaust
St Michael's Street, St Albans AL3 4SW
Tel: 01727 751810
www.stalbansmuseums.org.uk

Wardown Park Museum
Wardown Park, Luton LU2 7HA
Tel: 01582 546722
www.24hourrmuseum.org.uk

Wimpole Hall and Home Farm
Arrington, Royston SG8 0BW
Tel: 01223 206000
www.nationaltrust.org.uk

Wrest Park Gardens
Silsoe, Luton MK45 4HS
Tel: 01525 860152
www.english-heritage.org.uk

Arts and learning in Cambridgeshire and Bedfordshire

Anglesey Abbey, Garden and Lode Mill
Quy Road, Lode, Cambridge CB5 9EJ
Tel: 01223 810080
www.nationaltrust.org.uk

Bedford Museum
Castle Lane, Bedford MK40 3XD
Tel: 01234 353323
www.bedfordmuseum.org

Cambridge Botanic Garden
Cory Lodge, Bateman Street, Cambridge CB2 1JF
Tel: 01223 336265
www.botanic.cam.ac.uk

Cambridge and County Folk Museum
2/3 Castle Street, Cambridge CB3 0AQ
Tel: 01223 355159
www.folkmuseum.org.uk

Cecil Higgins Art Gallery
Castle Lane, Bedford MK40 3RP
Tel: 01234 211222
www.cecilhigginsartgallery.org

The English School of Falconry
Old Warden Park, Old Warden SG18 9ER
Tel 01767 627527
www.shuttleworth.org

The Fitzwilliam Museum
Trumpington Street, Cambridge CB2 1RB
Tel: 01223 332900
www.fitzmuseum.cam.ac.uk

Houghton Mill
Houghton, nr Huntingdon PE28 2AZ
Tel: 01480 301494
www.nationaltrust.org.uk

John Bunyan Museum and Library
Bunyan Meeting Free Church,
Mill Street, Bedford MK40 3EU
Tel: 01234 213722
www.bedfordmuseum.org

Leighton Buzzard Railway
Page's Park Station, Billington Road,
Leighton Buzzard LU7 4TN
Tel: 01525 373888
www.buzzrail.co.uk

Moggerhanger Park
Park Road, Moggerhanger MK44 3RW
Tel: 01767 641007
www.moggerhangerpark.com

Museum of Archaeology and Anthropology
Downing Street, Cambridge CB2 3DZ
Tel: 01223 333516
www.cam.ac.uk

Oliver Cromwell's House
29 St Mary's Street, Ely CB7 4HF
Tel: 01353 662062
www.eastcambs.gov.uk

Raptor Foundation
St Ives Road, Woodhurst PE28 3BT
Tel: 01487 741140
www.raptorfoundation.org.uk

St Neots Museum
The Old Court, 8 New Street,
St Neots PE19 8AE
Tel: 01480 388921
www.stneotsmuseum.org.uk

Scott Polar Research Institute Museum
Lensfield Road, Cambridge CB2 1ER
Tel: 01223 336540
www.spri.cam.ac.uk

Shuttleworth Collection
Old Warden Park, Old Warden,
Biggleswade SG18 9ER
Tel: 01767 627927
www.shuttleworth.org

The Stained Glass Museum
Ely Cathedral, Ely CB7 4DL
Tel: 01353 660347
www.stainedglassmuseum.com

Swiss Garden
Old Warden Park, Old Warden
Biggleswade SG18 9ER
Tel: 01767 627666
www.shuttleworth.org

Wicken Fen National Nature Reserve
Lode Lane, Wicken, Ely CB7 5XP
Tel: 01353 720274
www.nationaltrust.org.uk

Woburn Abbey
Woburn MK17 9WA
Tel: 01525 290333
www.woburnabbey.co.uk

Woburn Safari Park
Woburn MK17 9WA
Tel: 01525 290407
www.woburnsafari.co.uk

Wolds, Fens and sweeping skies

Battle of Britain Memorial Flight Visitor Centre
RAF Coningsby, Coningsby LN4 4SY
Tel: 01526 344041
www.lincolnshire.gov.uk

Belton House
Grantham NG32 2LS
Tel: 01476 566116
www.nationaltrust.org.uk

Boston Guildhall Museum
South Street, Boston PE21 6HT
Tel: 01205 365 954
www.lincolnshire.gov.uk

Cogglesford Watermill
East Road, Sleaford
Tel: 01529 400634
www.sleaforduk.com

Cranwell Aviation Heritage Centre
Heath Farm, North Rauceby, Cranwell, NG34 8QR
Tel: 01529 488490
www.lincolnshire.gov.uk

Gibraltar Point National Nature Reserve
Gibraltar Road, Skegness PE24 4SU
Tel: 01754 762677
www.lincstrust.org.uk

The Hub
Navigation Wharf, Carre Street NG34 7TW
Tel: 01529 308710
www.thehubcentre.org

Lincoln Castle
Castle Hill, Lincoln LN1 3AA
Tel: 01522 511068
www.lincolnshire.gov.uk

Lincoln Cathedral
Lincoln LN2 1PX
Tel: 01522 544544
www.lincolncathedral.com

Louth Museum
4 Broadbank, Louth LN11 0EQ
Tel: 01507 601211
www.lincolnshire.gov.uk

Maud Foster Windmill
Willoughby Road, Boston PE21 9EG
Tel: 01205 352188
www.lincolnshire.gov.uk

Museum of Lincolnshire Life
Burton Road, Lincoln LN1 3LY
Tel: 01522 528448
www.lincolnshire.gov.uk

Navigation House
Navigation Wharf, Carre Street, Sleaford NG34 7TW
Tel: 01529 414294
www.n-kesteven.gov.uk

Springfields Festival Gardens
Camelgate, Spalding PE12 6ET
Tel: 01775 724843
www.springfieldsgardens.co.uk

Tattershall Castle
Tattershall, Lincoln LN4 4LR
Tel: 01526 342543
www.nationaltrust.org.uk

Usher Gallery (The Collection)
Lindum Road, Lincoln LN2 1NN
Tel: 01522 527980
www.thecollection.lincoln.museum

Nottinghamshire: the heart of merrie England

Belvoir Castle
Belvoir, nr Grantham NG32 1PE
Tel: 01476 871002
www.belvoircastle.com

Clumber Park
Clumber Park, Worksop S80 3AZ
Tel: 01909 544917 (Infoline)
www.nationaltrust.org.uk

D H Lawrence Birthplace Museum
8a Victoria Street, Eastwood NG16 3AW
Tel: 01773 717353
www.broxstowe.gov.uk

Durban House Heritage Centre
Mansfield Road, Eastwood NG16 3DZ
Tel: 01773 717 353
www.broxstowe.gov.uk

Galleries of Justice
High Pavement, The Lace Market,
Nottingham NG1 1HN
Tel: 0115 952 0555
www.galleriesofjustice.org.uk

Hardwick Hall
Doe Lea, Chesterfield S44 5QJ
Tel: 01246 850430
www.nationaltrust.org.uk

Mr Straw's House
7 Blyth Grove, Worksop S81 0JG
Tel: 01909 482380
www.nationaltrust.org.uk

Millgate Museum
48 Millgate, Newark NG24 4TS
Tel: 01636 655730
www.newark-sherwooddc.gov.uk

Newark Air Museum
The Airfield, Winthorpe, Newark NG24 2NY
Tel: 01636 707170
www.newarkairmuseum.co.uk

Newstead Abbey
Newstead Abbey Park, Ravenshead NG15 8NA
Tel: 01623 455900
www.newsteadabbey.org.uk

Nottingham Castle Museum and Art Gallery
Friar Lane, off Maid Marian Way,
Nottingham NG1 6EL
Tel: 0115 915 3700.
www.nottinghamcity.gov.uk

Nottingham Caves
Broadmarsh Shopping Centre,
Nottingham NG1 7LS
Tel: 01159 520 555
www.nottinghamcity.gov.uk

Nottingham Transport Heritage Centre
Rushcliffe Country Park, Mere Way,
Ruddington, Nottingham
Tel: 0115 921 5705
www.rushcliffe.gov.uk

Sherwood Forest Country Park and Visitor Centre
Edwinstowe, Mansfield
Tel: 01623 823202
www.nottinghamshire.gov.uk

Sherwood Forest Farm Park
Lamb Pens Farm, Edwinstowe NG21 9HL
Tel: 01623 823 558
www.sherwoodforestfarmpark.co.uk

Thrumpton Hall
Thrumpton NG11 0AX
Tel: 01159 830410
www.thrumptonhall.com

Vina Cooke Museum of Dolls and Bygone Childhood
The Old Rectory, Great North Road,
Cromwell NG23 6JE
Tel: 01636 821364
www.nottinghamshire.gov.uk

Wollaton Hall and Park
Wollaton, Nottingham NG8 2AE
Tel: 0115 9153900

Canals, lakes and country estates in Leicestershire and Rutland

Barnsdale Gardens
The Avenue, Exton, Oakham LE15 8AH
Tel: 01572 813200
www.barnsdalegardens.co.uk

Battlefield Railway Line
Shackerstone Station, Shackerstone CB13 6NW
Tel: 01827 880754
www.battlefield-line-railway.co.uk

Bosworth Battlefield Visitor Centre and Country Park
Sutton Cheney CV13 0AD
Tel: 01455 290429
www.leics.gov.uk

Burghley House
Stamford PE9 2LQ
Tel: 01780 752451
www.burghley.co.uk

Conkers
Rawdon Road, Moira, Swadlincote DE12 6GA
Tel: 01283 216633
www.visitconkers.com

Foxton Canal Museum
Middle Lock, Gumley Road, Foxton LE16 7RA
Tel: 0116 2792657
www.fipt.org.uk

Great Central Railway
Great Central Station, Loughborough LE11 1RW
Tel: 01509 230726
www.gcrailway.co.uk

Harborough Museum
Council Offices, Adam and Eve Street,
Market Harborough LE16 7AG
Tel: 01858 821087
www.leics.gov.uk

Melton Carnegie Museum
Thorpe End, Melton Mowbray LE13 1RB
Tel: 01664 569946
www.leics.gov.uk

Oakham Castle
Oakham LE15 6HW
Tel: 01572 758440
www.rutnet.co.uk

Rockingham Castle
Rockingham, LE16 8TH
Tel: 01536 770240
www.rockinghamcastle.com

Rutland County Museum
Catmose Street, Oakham LE15 6HW
Tel: 01572 758440
www.rutnet.co.uk

Shackerstone Railwayana Museum
Shackerstone Station, Shackerstone CB13 6NW
Tel: 01827 880754
www.battlefield-line-railway.co.uk

Stamford Museum
Broad Street, Stamford PE9 1PJ
Tel: 01780 766317
www.leics.gov.uk

Northamptonshire: squires and spires

Althorp
Northampton NN7 4HQ
Tel: 01604 770107
www.althorp.com

Coton Manor Garden
Coton, nr Guilsborough NN6 8RQ
Tel: 01604 740219
www.cotonmanor.co.uk

Deene Park
Corby NN17 3EW
Tel: 01780 450278
www.deenepark.com

The Guildhall Visitor Centre
St Giles Square, Northampton
Tel: 01604 838800
www.northamptonboroughcouncil.com

Holdenby House
Northampton NN6 8DJ
Tel: 01604 770074
www.holdenby.com

Kirby Hall
Deene, Corby NN17 5EN
Tel: 01536 203230
www.english-heritage.org.uk

Naseby Battle and Farm Museum
Purlieu Farm, Naseby
www.hillyer.demon.co.uk

Northampton Museum and Art Gallery
Guildhall Road, Northampton NN1 1DP
Tel: 01604 838111
www.northampton.gov.uk

**Northamptonshire Ironstone
Railway Trust**
Hunsbury Hill Country Park, Hunsbury Hill
Road, Camp Hill, Northampton NN49UW
Tel: 01604 702031
www.nirt.co.uk

Rushton Triangular Lodge
Rushton NN14 1RP
Tel: 01536 710761
www.english-heritage.org.uk

Stoke Bruerne Canal Museum
Bridge Road, Stoke Bruerne, NN12 7SE
Tel: 01604 862229
www.thewaterwaystrust.org.uk

Stoke Park Pavilions
Stoke Bruerne, Towcester NN12 7RZ
Tel: 01604 862172

Windsor and the royal reaches of the Thames

Chinnor and Princes Risborough Railway
Chinnor Station, Station Road,
Chinnor OX39 4ER
Tel: 01844 353535
www.cprra.co.uk

Cliveden
Taplow, Maidenhead SL6 0JA
01628 605069
www.nationaltrust.org.uk

Eton College
Windsor SL4 6DW
Tel: 01753 671177
www.etoncollege.com

Hell Fire Caves
West Wycombe HP14 3AJ
Tel: 01494 533739
www.hellfirecaves.co.uk

Hughenden Manor
High Wycombe HP14 4LA
Tel: 01494 755565
www.nationaltrust.org.uk

Savill Garden
The Great Park,
Windsor SL4 2HT.
Tel 01753 847518
www.savillgarden.co.uk

West Wycombe Park
West Wycombe HP14 3AJ
Tel: 01494 513569
www.nationaltrust.org.uk

Windsor Castle
Windsor SL4 1NJ
Tel: 020 7766 7304
www.royalcollection.org

Oxford: city of dreaming spires and beyond

Abingdon Museum
The County Hall, Market Place
Abingdon OX14 3HG
Tel: 01235 523703
www.abingdon.gov.uk

Ashmolean Museum
Beaumont Street, Oxford OX1 2PH
Tel: 01865 278000
www.ashmol.ox.ac.uk

Beale Park
Lower Basildon, Reading RG8 9NH
Tel: 0870 7777160
www.bealepark.co.uk

Bodleian Library
Broad Street, Oxford OX1 3BG
Tel: 01865 277216
www.bodley.ox.ac.uk

Didcot Railway Centre
Didcot OX11 7NJ
Tel: 01235 817200
www.didcotrailwaycentre.org.uk

Mapledurham House and Mill
Mapledurham, Reading RG4 7TR
Tel: 0118 972 3350
www.mapledurham.co.uk

Oxford University Museum of Natural History
Parks Road, Oxford OX1 3PW
Tel: 01865 272950
www.oum.ox.ac.uk

Pitt Rivers Museum
South Parks Road, Oxford OX1 3PP
Tel: 01865 270927
www.prm.ox.ac.uk

River and Rowing Museum
Mill Meadows, Henley-on-Thames RG9 1BF
Tel: 01491 415600
www.rrm.co.uk

Stonor Park
Henley on Thames RG9 6HF
Tel: 01491 638587
www.stonor.com

Vale and Downland Museum
Church Street, Wantage OX12 8BL
Tel: 01235 771447
www.wantage.com

The Cherwell Valley and the Vale of Aylesbury: a retreat of millionaires

Ascott
Wing, nr Leighton Buzzard LU7 0PS
Tel: 01296 688242
www.nationaltrust.org.uk

Banbury Museum
Spiceball Park Road, Banbury OX16 2PQ
Tel: 01295 259855
www.cherwell-dc.gov.uk

Blenheim Palace
Woodstock OX20 1PX
Tel: 08700 602080
www.blenheimpalace.com

Boarstall Duck Decoy
Boarstall, nr Aylesbury HP18 9UX
Tel: 01844 237488
www.nationaltrust.org.uk

Broughton Castle
Broughton, Banbury OX15 5EB
Tel: 01295 276070
www.broughtoncastle.demon.uk

Claydon House
Middle Claydon, nr Buckingham MK18 2EY
Tel: 01494 755561
www.nationaltrust.org.uk

The Old Gaol Museum
Market Hill, Buckingham, MK18 1JX
Tel: 01280 823020
www.mkheritage.co.uk

The Oxfordshire Museum
Fletcher's House, Park Street
Woodstock OX20 1SN
Tel: 01993 811456
www.oxfordshire.gov.uk

Rousham House and Garden
nr Steeple Aston, Bicester OX25 4QX
Tel: 01869 347110
www.rousham.org

Sulgrave Manor
Manor Road, Sulgrave
nr Banbury OX17 2SD
Tel: 01295 760205
www.sulgravemanor.org.uk

Waddesdon Manor
Waddesdon, nr Aylesbury HP18 0JH
Tel: 01296 653211
www.nationaltrust.org.uk

The golden stone villages of the Cotswolds

Broadway Tower and Country Park
Broadway WR12 7LB
Tel: 01386 852390
www.thisisthecotswolds.co.uk

Chastleton House
Chastleton, nr Moreton-in-Marsh GL56 0SU
Tel: 01494 755560
www.nationaltrust.org.uk

Cheltenham Art Gallery and Museum
Clarence Street, Cheltenham GL50 3JT
Tel: 01242 237431
www.cheltenhammuseum.org.uk

Corinium Museum
Park Street, Cirencester GL7 2BX
Tel: 01285 655 611
www.cotswold.gov.uk

Hailes Abbey
nr Winchcombe, Cheltenham GL54 5PB
Tel: 01242 602398
www.nationaltrust.org.uk

Holst Birthplace Museum
4 Clarence Road, Pittville,
Cheltenham GL52 2AY
Tel: 01242 524846
www.holstmuseum.org.uk

Pittville Pump Room
Pittville Park, Cheltenham GL52 3JE
Tel: 01242 523852
www.cheltenham.gov.uk

Rodmarton Manor
Cirencester GL7 6PF
Tel: 01285 841253
www.rodmarton-manor.co.uk

Snowshill Manor
Snowshill, nr Broadway WR12 7JU
Tel: 01386 852410
www.nationaltrust.org.uk

Stanway House and Baroque Water Garden
Stanway, Cheltenham GL54 5PQ
Tel: 01386 584469
www.gloucestershire.gov

Sudeley Castle
Winchcombe, Cheltenham GL54 5JD
Tel: 01242 602308
www.sudeleycastle.co.uk

Tolsey Museum
126 High Street, Burford OX18 4QU
Tel: 01993 823236
www.oxfordshirecotswolds.org

Rustic charm in the Severn Valley

Berkeley Castle
Berkeley GL13 9BQ
Tel: 01453 810332
www.berkeley-castle.com

Clearwell Caves and Ancient Iron Mines
nr Coleford, Forest of Dean GL16 8JR
Tel: 01594 832535
www.clearwellcaves.com

Dean Heritage Centre
Camp Mill, Soudley,
Forest of Dean GL14 3JS
Tel: 01594 822170
www.deanheritagemuseum.com

Gloucester Cathedral
Gloucester GL1 2LR
Tel: 01452 528095
www.gloucestercathedral.org.uk

House of the Tailor of Gloucester
9 College Court, Gloucester GL1 2NJ
Tel: 01452 422856
www.gloucester.gov.uk

The Jenner Museum
Church Lane, Berkeley GL13 9BH
Tel: 01453 810631
www.jennermuseum.com

The Museum in the Park
Stratford Park, Stroud GL5 4AF
Tel: 01453 763394
www.stroud.gov.uk

National Waterways Museum,
Llanthony Warehouse, Gloucester Docks,
Gloucester GL1 2EH.
Tel: 01452 318200
www.nwm.org.uk

Owlpen Manor
nr Uley GL11 5BZ
Tel: 01453 860261
www.owlpen.com

Painswick Rococo Garden
Painswick GL6 6TH
Tel: 01452 813204
www.rococogarden.org.uk

Prinknash Abbey
Cranham GL4 8EX
Tel: 01452 812455
www.prinknashabbey.org.uk

Slimbridge Wildfowl and Wetlands Trust
Dursley GL2 7BT
Tel: 01453 890333
www.wwt.org.uk

Westbury Court Garden
Westbury-on-Severn GL14 1PD
Tel: 01452 760461
www.nationaltrust.org.uk

Westonbirt, the National Arboretum
Tetbury GL8 8QS
Tel: 01666 880220
www.forestry.gov.uk

Around Stratford-upon-Avon: in the footsteps of the Bard

The Almonry Museum and Heritage Centre
Abbey Gate, Evesham WR11 4BG
Tel: 01386 446 944
www.vehs.org.uk

Anne Hathaway's Cottage
Cottage Lane, Shottery CV37 9HH
Tel: 01789 292100
www.shakespeare.org.uk

Avoncroft Museum of Buildings
Stoke Heath, Bromsgrove B60 4JR
Tel: 01527 831886
www.avoncroft.org.uk

Charlecote Park
Warwick CV35 9ER
Tel: 01789 470277
www.nationaltrust.org.uk

Coughton Court
Alcester B49 5JA
Tel: 01789 400777
www.nationaltrust.org.uk

Hall's Croft
Old Town, Stratford-upon-Avon
CV37 6BG
Tel: 01789 204016
www.shakespeare.org.uk

Harvard House and the Museum of British Pewter
High Street, Stratford-upon-Avon
CV37 6AU
Tel: 01789 204507
www.shakespeare.org.uk

Lord Leycester Hospital
High Street, Warwick CV34 4BH
Tel: 01926 491422
www.warwick-uk.co.uk

Market Hall Museum
Market Place, Warwick CV34 4SA
Tel: 01926 412500
www.warwickshire.gov.uk

Mary Arden's House and Shakespeare's Countryside Museum
Station Road, Wilmcote CV37 9UN
Tel: 01789 293455
www.shakespeare.org.uk

Middle Littleton Tithe Barn
Middle Littleton, Evesham
Tel: 01905 371006
www.nationaltrust.org.uk

New Place/Nash's House
Chapel Street, Stratford-upon-Avon
CV37 6EP
Tel: 01789 292325
www.shakespeare.org.uk

Ragley Hall
Alcester B49 5NJ
Tel: 01789 762090
www.ragleyhall.com

Royal Shakespeare Theatre
Waterside, Stratford-upon-Avon CV37 6BB
Tel: 01789 403444
www.rsc.org.uk

St John's House Museum
St John's, Warwick CV34 4NF
Tel: 01926 412021/412132
www.warwickshire.gov.uk

Shakespeare's Birthplace and the Shakespeare Centre
Henley Street, Stratford-upon-Avon CV37 6QW
Tel: 01789 204016
www.shakespeare.org.uk

The Swan Theatre
Waterside, Stratford-upon-Avon CV37 6BB
Tel: 01789 403444
www.rsc.org.uk

Warwick Castle
Warwick CV34 4QU
Tel: 0870 4422000
www.warwick-castle.co.uk

Warwickshire Yeomanry Museum
The Court House, Jury Street,
Warwick CV34 4EW
Tel: 01926 494837
www.warwick-uk.co.uk

Warwickshire: from royal spa to classic cars

Baddesley Clinton Hall
Rising Lane, Baddesley Clinton,
Knowle, Solihull B93 0DQ
Tel: 01564 783294
www.nationaltrust.org.uk

The Herbert Art Gallery and Museum
Jordan Well, Coventry CV1 5QP
Tel: 024 7683 2386
www.theherbert.org

Heritage Motor Centre
Banbury Road, Gaydon CV35 0BJ
Tel: 01926 641188
www.heritage-motor-centre.co.uk

Kenilworth Castle
Castle Green, Kenilworth CV8 1NE
Tel: 01926 852078
www.english-heritage.org.uk

National Motorcycle Museum
Coventry Road, Bickenhill, Solihull B92 0EJ
Tel: 01675 443311
www.nationalmotorcyclemuseum.co.uk

Priory Visitor Centre
Priory Row, Coventry CV1 5EX
Tel: 024 7655 2242
www.theherbert.org

The Royal Pump Rooms
The Parade, Royal Leamington Spa
CV32 4AB
Tel: 01926 742762
www.royal-pump-rooms.co.uk

Rugby Art Gallery and Museum
Little Elborow Street, Rugby CV21 3AW
Tel: 01788 533201
www.rugby.gov.uk

Rugby School Museum
10 Little Church Street, Rugby CV21 3AW
Tel: 01788 556109
www.rugbyschool.net

St Michael's Cathedral
Coventry CV1 5AB
Tel: 024 7652 1200
www.coventrycathedral.org.uk

Stoneleigh Abbey
Kenilworth CV8 2LF
Tel: 01926 858535
www.stoneleighabbey.org

The Webb Ellis Rugby Football Museum
5 St Matthews Street, Rugby CV21 3BY
Tel: 01788 567777
www.rugby.gov.uk

Worcestershire: land of hope and glory

The Commandery
Sidbury, Worcester WR1 2HU
Tel: 01905 361821
www.worcestercitymuseums.org.uk

Droitwich Spa Heritage Centre
St Richard's House, Victoria Square,
Droitwich Spa WR9 8DS
Tel: 01905 774 312

Elgar Birthplace Museum
Crown East Lane, Lower Broadheath WR2 6RH
Tel: 01905 333224
www.elgarmuseum.org

Great Malvern Priory
Church Street, Malvern
Tel: 01684 561020
www.malvern.whub.org.uk

The Greyfriars
Friar Street, Worcester WR1 2LZ
Tel: 01905 23571
www.nationaltrust.org.uk

Harvington Hall
Harvington Hall Lane,
Harvington DY10 4LR
Tel: 01562 777846
www.harvingtonhall.com

The King Charles House
New Street, Worcester
Tel: 01905 22449

Lower Brockhampton House
Bringsty, Worcester WR6 5TB
Tel: 01885 482077
www.nationaltrust.org.uk

Pershore Abbey
Church Street, Pershore WR10 1DT
Tel: 01386 561520
www.pershoreabbey.fsnet.co.uk

Priory House
Friar Street, Droitwich WR9 8ED
Tel: 01905 773370

Royal Worcester
Severn Street, Worcester WR1 2NE
Tel: 01905 746000
www.royal-worcester.co.uk

Severn Valley Railway
The Railway Station, Bewdley DY12 1BG
Tel: 01299 403816
www.svr.co.uk

Spetchley Park and Gardens
Worcester WR5 1RS
Tel: 01453 810303
www.spetchleygardens.co.uk

The Tudor House
16 Church Street, Upton-Upon-Severn
WR8 0HT
Tel: 01684 592447
www.worcestershire.whub.org.uk

The Upton Heritage Centre
The Pepperpot, Church Street,
Upton-upon-Severn WR8 0HT
Tel: 01684 592679
www.worcestershire.whub.org.uk

Witley Court
Great Witley WR6 6JT
Tel: 01299 896636
www.english-heritage.org.uk

Worcester Cathedral
Worcester WR1 2LH
Tel: 01905 28854
www.cofe-worcester.org.uk

Worcestershire County Museum
Hartlebury Castle, Hartlebury DY11 7XZ
Tel: 01299 250416
www.worcestershire.gov.uk

Herefordshire's black-and-white villages and the Golden Valley

Abbey Dore Court Garden
Abbey Dore, Hereford HR2 0AD
Tel: 01981 240419
www.abbeydorecourt.co.uk

Burton Court
Eardisland HR6 9DN
Tel: 01544 388231
www.burtoncourt.com

Butcher's Row House Museum
Church Lane, Ledbury HR8 1DW
Tel: 01531 632040

Hereford Cathedral
Hereford HR1 2NG
Tel: 01432 374200
www.herefordcathedral.org

Hereford Cider Museum and King Offa Distillery
21 Ryelands Street, Hereford HR4 0LW
Tel: 01432 354207
www.cidermuseum.co.uk

Hereford Museum and Art Gallery
Broad Street, Hereford HR4 9AU
Tel: 01432 260692
www.herefordshire.gov.uk

Hergest Croft Gardens
Kington HR5 3EG
Tel: 01544 230160
www.hergest.co.uk

Shropshire: birthplace of the Industrial Revolution

Acton Burnell Castle
Acton Burnell, Shrewsbury
Tel: 0121 625 6820
www.english-heritage.org.uk

Acton Scott Working Farm Museum
Wenlock Lodge, Acton Scott,
Church Stretton SY6 6QN
Tel: 01694 781306
www.actonscottmuseum.co.uk

Attingham Park
Atcham, Shrewsbury SY4 4TP
Tel: 01743 708123
www.nationaltrust.org.uk

Bridgnorth Castle
Castle Hill, Bridgnorth
Tel: 01746 762231
www.shropshiretourism.info

Bridgnorth Cliff Railway
6a Castle Terrace, Bridgnorth WV16 4AH
Tel: 01746 762052
www.bridgnorthcliffrailway.co.uk

Buildwas Abbey
Ironbridge, Telford TF8 7BW
Tel: 01952 433274
www.english-heritage.org.uk

Castle Lodge
Castle Square, Ludlow SY8 1AY
Tel: 01584 878098

Clun Museum
Town hall, Clun SY7 8JA
Tel: 01588 640681
www.southshropshire.org.uk

The Ironbridge Gorge Museums
Coach Road, Coalbrookdale TF8 7DQ
Tel: 01952 884391
www.ironbridge.org.uk

Ludlow Castle
Castle Square, Ludlow SY8 1AY
Tel: 01584 873355
www.ludlowcastle.com

Secret Hills Discovery Centre
School Road, Craven Arms SY7 9RS
Tel: 01588 676000
www.shropshirehillsdiscoverycentre.co.uk

The Shropshire Regimental Museum
Shrewsbury Castle, Shrewsbury SY1 2AT
Tel: 01743 262292
www.shropshiremuseums.com

Shrewsbury Castle and Shropshire Regimental Museum
Castle Street, Shrewsbury SY1 2AT
Tel: 01743 361196
www.shrewsburymuseums.com

Shrewsbury Museum and Art Gallery
Rowley's House, Barker Street,
Shrewsbury SY1 1QH
Tel: 01743 361196
www.shrewsburymuseums.com

Stokesay Castle
Craven Arms SY7 9AH
Tel: 01588 672544
www.english-heritage.org.uk

Viroconium Roman City
Wroxeter, Shrewsbury SY5 6PH
Tel: 01743 761330
www.english-heritage.org.uk

Index

Credits

t = top; tl= top left; top centre = tc; top right = tr; centre = c; centre above = ca; centre below = cb; bottom= b; bottom left = bl; bottom centre = bc; bottom right = br

VisitBritain would like to thank the following for their assistance with photographic material for this publication:
firstsite, contemporary art Colchester 33b; Great Central Railway 69b; Herefordshire Council 127cb, 131c; Henry Moore Foundation – The work illustrated on p43tl has been reproduced by permission of the Henry Moore Foundation, photo: Michel Muller; Sabine J Hutchinson – www.photographybysabine.co.uk 134b; Lisa Kosky 12t, 18bl; Leicester Shire Promotions Ltd 64bl, 64br, 65b, 67tl, 69ca, 69cb; Photographs reproduced with kind permission of the Museum of East Anglian Life 31b; National Trust Picture Library/Andrew Butler 97tr, /Colin Clarke 91t, /Geoffrey Frosh 63t, /John Hammond 92b, /Nick Meers 17br; Northampton Tourist Information Centre 70t, 71b, 71c, Rugby School 116cb, Science and Society Picture Library 56t, Vale of White Horse District Council 87b, Warwick Castle 114b, Worcestershire County Museum 125t

All remaining photographs have been sourced from VisitBritain's online picture library (www.britainonview.com) with credits to:
Tim Fox jacket
David Ashwin 59b; Keyna Doran 98tl; Rod Edwards 6–7, 14b, 16t, 32t, 34t, 37t, 45t, 47b, 55t, 55b, 95t; David Hall 105t; David Hunter 105b, 112t, 124t Rob Judges 83t; Dr Trevor Kerry 52t; Martin Knight 59t; Pawel Libera 104–5; Tom McGahan 36tl; Kathy Mansfield 85b, 86t; John Miller 10–11, 25c; Dave Porter 71t; David Sellman 23t, 99tl; Jill Swainson 113cb; TNT/Eric Nathan 62b; V K Guy Ltd/Mike Guy 25t, /Vic Guy 82–3, 90b; Roy Westlake 85t; John Whitaker 32–33c, 33t, 44–5, 53t

Design: Clare Thorpe, Janis Utton
Editor: Debbie Woska
Index: Hilary Bird
Picture research: Rebecca Shoben
Proof reader: Gary Werner